QUALITY OF WORKING LIFE OF WOMEN CONSTRUCTION WORKERS

QUALITY OF WORKING LIFE OF WOMEN CONSTRUCTION WORKERS

R.N. MATHUR

Commonwealth

Quality of Working Life of Women Construction Workers

Edition : 2022

ISBN : 81-7169-000-9

Published by :
COMMONWEALTH PUBLISHERS (P) LTD.
4831/24, Govind Lane,
Ansari Road, Darya Ganj,
New Delhi - 110002
Ph. : 23272541, 23242541
e-mail : commonwealthpublishers2016@gmail.com

Distributed by :
ARJUN PUBLISHING HOUSE
4831/24, Govind Lane,
Ansari Road, Darya Ganj,
New Delhi - 110002
Ph. : 23272541, 23242541
e-mail : arjunbooks2001@gmail.com

Laser Typesetting by :
Dimple Computers
Delhi

Printed at :
Milan Enterprises
Delhi

Dedicated to my Parents

Foreword

Women throughout the world, have been considered as weaker sex whereas, in many spheres of economic, scientific and technological activities their contribution is not a shade less than that of the opposite sex'. Patriarchal domination in *most societies of the world has suppressed* womens image, role and contribution to such an extent that it has become a habit to consider women as misfit, more so due to technological advancements in different walks of life. This even led to misperceptions of women by themselves too, of their own life, *self image, self respect* and even *self confidence.* It is not only a social manifestation but even in the world of work, women continue to have similar misperceptions. Heavy industrialization and introduction of technologies in the world of work have further weakened women's position. For a long time they had no proper exposure to working opportunities, better education to reach higher levels in society and acquisition of skills to meet the requirements of handling scientific and technological equipment and instruments.

The condition of women in the world has further deteriorated. The year 1975 was declared "Women Liberation Year" by the United Nations. The Government of India also constituted a National Committee to ascertain status of women in India. The Committee identified several problems, issues and drudgery faced by women and recommended several measures to uplift women from their poor status and join the main stream of the country and contribute significantly to the economy.

It could be said that women in organised sectors are still in 'Controlled Situation' and by adopting effective policies better opportunities for women could be created. But women in unorganized sectors such as construction could be defined as the oppressed section of society by ascertaining just one fact that not a single woman in the country possessed construction skills. The Government, even after realizing the status of women in construction industry, has not opened any institution or course or programme in any part of the country which could provide construction skill development opportunities to women workers.

On each construction site about 25 per cent of the labourers are women who work and live under sub-dued conditions with family and children, without proper living facilities, working conditions, certain times unequal wages and receive humiliating treatment from contractors etc. On top of it, their employment is seasonal and their own background is based on rural value system as their basic economic category is that of landless labourers who come from rural areas to cities in search of employment as a mass of illiterates with poor knowledge of urban life style.

However, many documents and studies have attempted to count actual number of construction workers in the country but all indicate different figures which proves that the actual number of construction workers is not known. The studies so far conducted have analysed demographic details of the workers in construction industry and many social service agencies like Mobile Creche have done appreciable work to provide support services specially to women construction workers but none of the studies have ever attempted to know the perception of the women construction worker about themselves, their work related aspects and living conditions which are the fundamental components of assessing quality of life. This book analyses in detail such assessments and has gone deep into the existing work motivation theories to assess "Conditions" and "Feelings" (postulates of Herzberg's theory of motivation) of the women construction workers. The theory of Maslow (1954) has been evaluated in the context and it has been observed that most of the women workers in construction industry strive for satisfaction of basic needs. The higher order needs such as esteem needs and self actualisation never appear in their life. So is true as per this investigation. For the last 40 to 50 years of my conscious observation of the women workers, the state of affairs has hardly changed. Women in this industry have been working for unskilled occupations for ages and have never been exposed to any opportunity of moving up in the ladder to obtain satisfaction of higher order needs.

This volume of work presents a number of eye opening facts, apart from the most revealing findings which need attention of the educational planners to cater to the needs of women construction workers and to devise a system of education and training which would be useful, specially for developing construction skills among women apart from acquiring functional literacy. The work would also be useful for law makers who of course, framed laws for providing equality to women in this sector but their enforcement is almost negligible and now need new set of effective laws.

I hope that the readers of this book would find in it positive contribution towards understanding the quality of working life (QWL) of women construction workers in a better way. From such understanding and only therefrom we can move towards effective policies, designed to modify quality of working life of these workers which will ultimately benefit increased flow of women workers in the construction industry to work on higher occupations than only labourers and reduce inequality and poverty.

I hope the efforts of Dr. R.N. Mathur will open avenues of correctives to alleviate the suffering of the mother source of humanity.

DR. V.N. VASHIST
Managing Director,
Educational Consultants India Ltd.,
(A Govt. of India Enterprise)
A-1/111, Safdarjung Enclave,
NEW DELHI-110 029

NEW DELHI
20-09-1989

Preface

The modern technology has brought in a variety of changes in the life style as well as working patterns of individuals which demand cognisation and adaptation to the changing environment both in social as well as working context. It is also necessary now a days to work as the economic pressure has increased so much that it demands contribution of both husband and wife. This factor is more apparent among low paid workers and calls for a new generation of workers comprising of women. It is not true to say that women are a new class of workers, women have been working since the emergence of human race but her contributions were not counted economically. Now in the industrial settings things have become more clear.

For earning basic subsistance human beings have to work and work under certain conditions which are generally aimed to attain cost effectiveness with minimum input. Such objectives if exercised in a disproportionate manner may create problems. One of such problem is feelings of the workers towards the conditions of work which are the basic causes of labour unrest.

In the organized sector, the situation is within controlled limits but as in India and most of the developing countries, there is unorganized sector growing parallely which to a great extent has dependence on organized sector. Out of many unorganized sectors in India, construction is one which contributes substantially to the economy and is next to the agriculture sector.

Women in construction industry have a typical status which has not changed to even apparenly significant extent in last one century. They have always worked as labours on unskilled ardous tasks and are forced to face enormous problems in both work settings and at home, performing dual task of child bearing and working for earning the subsistance for the family. The lack of medical facility, proper living space, knowledge of urban style of life and surroundings and many such factors force them to always strive for satisfaction of their basic needs and are never able to attain higher order needs such as esteem needs and self actualization.

The present investigation has of course made an initial attempt to explore relationship of various background variables work related variables, supervisory performance appraisal, and attitude towards education need fulfilment with Quality of Working Life (QWL). The findings have been dealt in details in various chapters of this book.

This work has included women workers of construction industry and that is the reason it has acquired a uniqueness. I feel privileged to state that it is the first doctoral dissertation in India, recognized by a premier institution like Indian Institute of Technology, Delhi on QWL of women construction workers. The work further needs to be extended and done repeatedly along with certain intervention programmes of education and training. The effect of such programmes should be studied on all the variables mentioned in the book and the programmes must be redesigned to become more effective.

Such an innovative and unique work is never possible untill and unless the support of experts in the field is not provided. In this context, I would feel proud and privileged in expressing my deep sense of gratitude to Prof. (Mrs) Poornima Mathur, Professor, Department of Humanities and

Social Sciences, Indian Institute of Technology, Delhi for inspiring guidance throughout the course of this insvestigation.

I am deeply indebted Dr. A.L. Ram for his personal and keen interest in my work. His criticisms and ideas provided valuable suggestions and new look to my work.

In the same vein I feel indebted to Dr (Miss) Sarojini Bisaria, NCERT, New Delhi and Shri G.C. Mathur, Former Director, National Buildings Organization, New Delhi who not only inspired and encouraged me but offered valuable suggestions to strengthen my work.

I must not forget to mention the contributions made by Shri Bishwa Prakash Nauriyal and Shri Devinder Kumar to help me collect the data from women workers. I would also like to thank my wife Mrs. Sunita Mathur, Educational Vocational Guidence Counsellor, Government Senior Secondary School, East of Kailash, New Delhi for her help and assistance which was all the time available to me.

I also received substantial support from my collegue researchers and friends to conduct the investigation. Specific to mention are Dr. A.D. Tiwari, Dr. G.C. Upadhyay, Dr. D.K. Sharma, Dr. Nagendra Singh, Shri Bijoy Panda and Shri C.D. Tiwari. I express my gratitude to them for their support.

Last but not the least I am greately indebted to all the women construction workers who provided me the information about their work and life without which this investigation would have never been possible and also those who directly and indirectly helped me to conduct data collection work which was the most difficult work of this investigation.

R.N. MATHUR

Contents

List of Tables

Figures

Photographs

1

Introduction

The advent of modern technology has penetrated into the day-to-day life of every individual, both in the working as well as household domain. Cognization and adaptation have led to striking changes in the life style and perception of life as a whole. This doctrine is applicable to people belonging to all sections of society. The change in the perception of life and adaptation to cope up with the change is specially evident in the elite class who have economic, social and psychological preparedness, but for those belonging to middle, low and still the deprived sections of society have yet to develop measures and means to cope up with the situation. They also sometimes consider it as an external force for which they are forced to adapt. These changes in the social structure and social practices leave behind enormous scope for social scientists to undertake micro-level researches to study the cause and effect relationship to develop newer strategies to decrease time lag between introduction of technology and adaptation.

Introduction of technology leads to hazardous changes in the employment structure of an organisation and the most affected are the workers at the grass-root level who have to immediately enter into competitive world of work for their survival and in the process the misfit is thrown out. The social misnormer is that it is generally the poor woman. In the male dominated society she is labelled as mentally incapable to be deserving to survive.

In the organised sector of industries, the situation may be controlled by the unions, but in the unorganised sectors such as construction, agriculture and domestic spheres, women are gradually becoming out of context. They are just left to be subjected to unskilled occupations and arduous jobs and inspite of interest, never get opportunity to be exposed to influences of skill development. In this situation, one can estimate the status and standard of the quality of working life which is further worsended by dual role performing. To work at home; bearing and care of young children, performing household chores are unescapable responsibilities for which no compensation is granted. To work out of home is embodied in the social stigma and women's economic contributions is considered secondary to men. The labour market studies, census and economic surveys do not recognise women as economic contributors.

To work is human nature and it has became a necessity because it yields money which is needed for basic survival in the context of today's world. Upon satisfaction of basic needs the work also provides opportunity to satisfy higher order needs which yields social prestige and development of excellence and expertise. If we evaluate the aforesaid statement in the context of women workers in the construction industry, who are considered as the lowest level of workers in the ladder of status and standard, the conclusions will be eye-opening. First, that the women workers are basically agriculture labour, migrating from drought-prone rural areas to urban cities in search of employment. The unorganised construction industry, being labour intensive, offers immediate employment. The legislative rights have been framed for such labours but their implementation is almost absent. Second, that since women do not have construction skills, are absorbed as unskilled labourers. There are no informal or institutional opportunities available to them for either functional education or vocational training. Third, that women are considered mentally incapable to understand the mysteries of technology and are misfits, hence, construction remains as a male dominated profession. Fourth, that in the urban life, women have to face many inadequacies. Lack of awareness of work laws and use of public facilities, education, vocational training and work experience, contribute lack of to exploitative situation. Fifth, that women have to live under subdued living conditions with no suitable places of public conveniences, small hutments, without street and lighting arrangements, security arrangements, ration cards, etc.

The aforesaid indicators are the conditions of their work and need attempts to know from the workers themselves about how they feel about each of them. So far, very few attempts have been made in this area out of these specific to mention are studies conducted by Indian Council of Social Science Research on women construction workers as a part of preparation of the report for the Committee on Status of Women in India (1975) and some census surveys of the centres run by Mobile Creches (1979). Both of these studies highlight objective indicators of quality of working life of the women workers. The subjective indicators i.e. feelings towards work conditions, are yet to attract attention of the researchers which seems to be the most important parameter of quality of working life specially of these workers.

Quality of working life is a recent concept for the behavioural scientists. The term was first coined by Davis in 1972 in an International Conference of Arden House, New York. The thought has then travelled through to be considered as a 'movement', 'reform' and 'policy' for increased productivity in an organisation (Promonis and Baumgratel, 1980). Carlson (1978) viewed quality of working life as both a goal and an ongoing process for achieving the same. Nadler and Lawler (1953) defined quality of working life as a 'variable' (1969-72), as a 'method' (1972-75), as a 'movement' (1975-80) and as 'everything' (1979-82). They ultimately defined quality of working life as a way of thinking about people, work and organisation. In fact, on the content aspect also researchers differ but it is clear that most of the investigations lay emphasis on only the work environment as the text of quality of working life, providing secondary importance to the living environment (Walker, 1975; Walton, 1975; Joseph, 1978; Mill, 1978). These studies have been conducted on high level workers, only Joseph (1978) collected data from skilled and semi-skilled workers and found that attitude towards nature of work is clearly associated with quality of working life, associates or co-workers have the potential to make quality of working life high or low and supervision and pay appear to be least associated with quality of working life. Ghosh and Kalra (1982), while studying quality of working life concluded that background variables are associated with quality of working life. Sayeed and Sinha (1981) worked with class III employees and stated that higher quality of working life leads to greater job satisfaction and performance.

The basic needs and insecurity of job dominate the behaviour of women workers. The workers also strive to earn a respectable self image in their society. The developmental opportunities in terms of skill enhancement are almost negligible. Maslow's theory (1954) has been evaluated by many researchers in organised industries but no significant attempt has been made to test validity of the theory in unorganised industries.

The women construction workers belong to low economic level and in the urban atmosphere their position is further lowered. The working and living conditions are not adequate. The availability of developmental opportunities are negligible. The unorganised character of construction industry call for attention of organisational researchers to conduct researches in the direction of human resource development so that this sector also acquires organised status and the labours get opportunities for self development and become more productive thereby enhancing their standard quality of life.

In the aforesaid context, the present study planned to explore various factors such as background variables, work related variables, living conditions, general awareness, attitude towards education, performance level assessment and need fulfilment and their relationship with quality of working life of the women workers in the construction industry. The study is an initial step towards an understanding of the quality of working life in the unorganised construction industry.

2

Quality of Working Life-Concept and Expressions

"Quality of Life" the Concerned Expression

Nobody seems to know who coined the word 'quality of life' which has lately achieved a remarkable popularity among the academic communities of social scientists and more specially among work oriented organisations and their managements. The same term is used differently in different languages in the developed countries and more often the term is used in complaints made by representatives of the developing countries in the United Nations about living conditions in their homeland.

Szalai (1978) approached eminent researchers, personally and through correspondence who were participants of two symposia devoted to the discussion, on various aspects of quality of life at the Ninth World Congress of Sociology (1978) at Uppsala. The attempt produced some evidences that the expression first came into light in the late 1950s or early 1960s but not in scholarly context, rather in newspapers or general publications mostly in connection with problems of environmental pollution, the deterioration of urban living conditions and the like. Szalai also scanned through 20 major encyclopaedias published uptil 1978 but he could not locate any mention or entry having quality of life 'as its subject or any direct or indirect reference. He then argued that the expression has basic orientation in day-to-day conversation questions "how are you?" which proves capability of human beings to keep in evidence of life, the conditions of their existence and to form integral judgement about their life. Therefore, the age old and uniquitous "how are you" type of questions have as their vaguely defined object, the expression of an interest in health, welfare and prosperity, in the goodness of life as the 'quality of life' of the person addressed.

Quality of life acquired sociological importance and became a topic of social research which converge largely on people's welfare and well being, their living conditions, their style of life, their standard of living. A new branch of socio-economic investigation took a formal shape called "study of social indicator system" and were applied in the processes of socio-economic planning, public policy decision making and even in marketing research.

Blishen and Atkinson (1978) also observed growing international concern about quality of life but stated that there was no agreement on specifying meanings of the term which resulted in differences in defining statistical indicators. Largely. two types of indicators come into picture about quality of life. Objective indicators, such as, money and subjective indicators, such as financial status, living standard, job etc. The objective indicators define the quality of life in terms of goods thought to constitute desired states of existence by Govt. agencies while the subjective indicators conceptualize individuals to define themselves, the quality of their life as perceived by them.

Hankiss (1978) pointed out that research work has revealed that quality of life is not simply the sum of its component units; it is much more than the resultant of interaction of welter of herogeneous forces and factors. And since, in the course of this interaction, the raw variables registered during the interviews undergo a thorough transformation, their ultimate meaning and significance can be determined only if they are analysed as the component parts of life-quality, considered as a coherent and integral system. Like Blishen and Atkinson he also argued that objective variables are concerned with the comparison of immediate surveys or census data which may allow important and valid inferences to the quality of life of the population. However, the immediate comparison of subjective variables, such as, attitudes, aspirations, fears, frustrations and satisfactions or dissatisfactions need more careful and controlled observation and infact with such indicators one can go beyond the surface registration of cross cultural similarities and dissimilarities.

A number of researches pertaining to problems regarding socialization and personality development have cleared the doubts that a strong and systematic relationship exists between the personalities of individuals and social structures that socialise and support them. General measures of socio-economic status have been shown powerfully to condition the attitudes and values of individuals, in particular, the degree of their authoritarianism (Lipset, 1960) their sense of personal efficiency, their satisfaction with their jobs and life situations (Inkeles, 1960), and the values around which they socialize their children (Pearlin and Kohn, 1966). The nature of the jobs men hold, especially the job's substantive complexity as well as feelings, powerlessness and self-estrangement (Kohn and Schooler, 1973 and Kohn, 1976).

In the late sixties and early seventies the behavioural scientists started looking at the concept as the subjective assessment was their own responsibility. It was believed that in objective indicators the parametres show unchanged structural features whereas in the subjective indicators there are fundamental differences about the way people arrive at the assessment of their well-being. With the argument certain models were developed to view 'quality of life' from a combination of factors which were *statistical and psychological.*

Abrams, 1973; Hall, 1976 in Britain, Andrews and Withey, 1976; Campbell et. al, 1976 in U.S A. and Blishen et. al, 1975 in Canada.

Rezsohazy (1978) also defined quality of life by calling it as ways of life and considered it as life style as an overall behaviour resultant of occasions like occurring daily (as at work) or seasonally (as vocations) or irregularly (as sickness) or even at unique occasions (such as marriage).

Stone (1978) in his theoretical paper on "organic solidarity and life quality indicators" accepted the importance of psychological factors in the assessment of quality of life. An individual has to consider the question of everything in terms of satisfying or frustrating. Certain satisfying things may become dissatisfying or frustrating at a span of time and one time scheduling may disrupt others resulting into frustration.

Solomon et.al. (1978) have pointed out that industrialisation has caused social and environmental disturbances. The declarations for improvement of quality of life of people as a national objective is easy to agree upon but there is little consensus on how the quality of life should be defined, measured and fostered ? According to them, quality of life is, therefore, both material satisfaction of vital needs and aspects of life such as personal development, self realisation and a balanced eco-system. They also believe that quality of life has objective and subjective components which define a unique way for improvement for different social groups, cultures and nations.

Many authors have defined human needs and proposed classification schemes (Bossel, 1976; Galtung, 1975; Hankiss, 1976; Jarett, 1976; Mallamann, 1977; Masini, 1975; Maslow, 1971; McHale et. al, 1977). All of these are attempts to determine the necessity and, if possible, independent needs in order to describe all possible human behaviours.

Verwayen (1978) has reported that the Organisation for Economic Cooperation and Development, Paris had initiated

Social Indicators Development Programme in some of the countries to measure quality of life on the assumption that similarities of well-being and methodological principles of these surveys will be constant for all the countries under study. The areas that have been selected for this intensive work were :

1. healthfulness of life,
2. measurement of learning,
3. employment,
4. quality of working life,
5. time and leisure,
6. income, wealth and material deprivation,
7. housing conditions,
8. quality of the natural environment,
9. measurement of victimization,
10. inequality,
11. economic accessibility,
12. comprehensive survey,
13. methodological issues in data collection,
14. presentation of social indicators and statistics, and
15. applicability of selected social concerns andindicators to particular national contexts. Sixteen projects were initiated and results of these studies are yet to be published.

Similarly, a number of other studies have highlighted various factors of quality of life which include work as most important aspect. The work provides a number of social material and psychological satisfactions because it largely yields money, either in the form of wages/pay or profits in a business organisation. Work has the potential to motivate individuals in numerous ways. What seems to be more important is an individual's perception of his work and his working life. This directly indicates existence of two types of factors, one related to the conditions of work and the other as to how the individual is perceiving these conditions of work to obstacle or facilitate his work output. At individual level working life and feelings towards work conditions determine his work environment and any improvement to it will lead to improvement in terms of total productivity.

Rise of QWL Movement

In the context of quality of life, researches have been done in abundance taking working life as one of the factors but, as an independent factor, quality of working life (QWL) acquired its importance very recently. The debate among scientists in various disciplines are putting forth their thoughts towards definition, measurement and effective utilisation of the concept in industrial settings.

The managers of the recent time have been confronted with various organisational problems, out of which the most crucial is labour problem because machines, materials and the energy to run the machines don't perceive their environment, only man or workers do perceive. A number of researches have helped in understanding the concept and other associated concepts which will be discussed to arrive at operational definition of the term for use in the present investigation.

Newly acquired economic maturity appears to be one of the causes of the increased concern for improving the quality of working life. In many societies the framework of problem awareness for evaluating work experience has changed. This new awareness is generally attributed to the hightened aspirations of workers with regard to their working life, aspirations which in turn have been affected by improving living standards and higher educational levels of the work force in general.

Many of the current, against traditional, problems are not the result of deteriorating social and working conditions rather, a consequence of hightened worker expectations and aspirations. Moreover, a number of aspects traditionally considered to be important are gradually giving way to new concerns.

New problems affecting the QWL, fall in several categories. Some have surfaced as a result of new technological and social developments, others represent changing and accelerating emphases on long recognised problem situations and conditions and still others relate to certain aspects of previously uncontested conditions which only recently have aroused concern regarding their compatibility with an acceptable level of QWL.

Walton (1975) pointed out that even though attention tends to be focussed on a few cases of obvious improvements which are widely publicised, demands for changes are usually not restricted to one or two aspects of the QWL. In fact, the extent of issues related to the QWL is as broad as the whole range of labour problems.

Although opinions remain divided, there is some proof that unfulfilled needs and demands may lead not only to worker dissatisfaction but also to alienation from work, low productivity and social instability.

Along with the individual differences in the perception of the QWL, there are also political, economic, social and cultural conditions which differ vastly among societies, they also result in widely varying degrees of problem consciousness and in different counter measures that have been devised in response to workers' needs that have recently emerged.

In the past few years, quality of working life has emerged as a central issue not only in India but also in other developed nations. The growing concern is evident from the growing number of national and international conferences of managers, union leaders, government officials and behavioural scientists. Perhaps the major cause for much of the recent concern is the alarm expressed by many about what has been termed the QWL problem facing today's workers and organisations. Yet there is currently a great deal of uncertainty and disagreement about just how serious this problem is, how widespread it is or whether it exists at all. Some argue that the problem is very real and very serious. Others view it as little more than the normal and expected growing pains of industry especially as maturity. Finally, still others view the quality of work life problem as one largely created by the media and little more than a passing interest.

There are few valid or conclusive data that speak directly to the existence, the seriousness or the scope of the quality of working life problem much less to its sources or its effects but the importance of the problem is perceived as serious by few duc to following reasons :

1. Worker alienation and job dissatisfaction are increasing primarily as a result of meaningless jobs and authoritarian superiors.
2. The productivity of workers and industry is declining while counter productive behaviours (such as, sabotage, strikes, absenteeism, union militancy or alcoholism at work) are increasing.
3. The confidence of the public in large institutions in general and big businesses in particular is eroding.

The surveys conducted earlier shows that the behaviours like absenteeism, turn-over, job satisfaction and productivity are partially influenced by quality of working life. The reason is that while all of these attitudes or behaviours are indeed influenced by QWL, each are influenced by other factors as well. The other factors are : individual's expectations and values as well as what happens at work, technology, skills as well as motivation, etc.

Quality of working life is both a good and on-going process for achieving it. As a goal, QWL is the commitment of any organisation to work improvement, the creation of more involving, satisfying and effective jobs and work environment for people at all levels of the organisation. As a process, QWL calls for efforts to realise this goal through the active involvement of people throughout the organisation. As a result of their involvement, people can make more meaningful contributions to the organisation, its objectives and its ability to cope with the changing demands of a changing environment and at the same time, experience greater feelings of satisfaction, pride in accomplishment and personal growth. Importantly, QWL brings together the needs and development of people with the goals and development of the organisation.

QWL is also a philosophy and a concept of management. The philosophy is broad, many facetted and varying somewhat in its specific form, one culture to the next or from one organisation to other within the same organisation. But the basic idea is same, a climate must be encouraged in which the fundamental human dignity of all members of the organisation are recognised, not only because they are entitled to it but also because workers are the most critical assets to the organisation and its future.

In France, when the main employers' and workers' organisations decided in 1973 to launch inter-industry negotiations upon "working conditions", the issues to be discussed were classified under these headings: work organisation; organisation of working time; payment by results; health and safety; and the role of supervisory staff.

All these considerations lead to the view that the concept of quality of working life should first be used in its broad sense in order to examine the total labour problems of each society. First, on the basis of past and present economic conditions of each nation, one can judge the areas in which meaningful improvements can realistically be made and at what level. Secondly, the socio-cultural background of society helps to define not only what goals should be selected but how they should be pursued.

Inspite of the great variety of economic, social, cultural and political situations in industrial societies, there is a broadly shared conviction that coherent and multi-facetted national policies are needed for the improvement of working conditions and of the quality of life. There is no doubt that increased protection of the physical and social working environment, new working time arrangements, improved pay systems, new and imaginative ways of organising work, wider application of ergonomics, and increased participation of workers in decisions directly affecting their working life. All these can make a substantial contribution to eliminating outdated and harmful methods of work and help promoting the QWL.

The continuous rise in material living standards tended to fulfil workers' need to achieve on the one hand power and equity and on the other prosperity. The goal of these workers began to rise higher and also to develop in a variety of directions. The relaxation of social control made it possible for them to express overtly their needs and problems, and to pursue personal satisfaction more directly. This liberation entailed first a general elevation of the level of aspirations, from material to psychological and from immediate to long range.

The internal work environment within the organisation began to prove inadequate in the light of new worker values. Many of the previously accepted technical, organisational and social assumptions of organizations began to cause disfunctional symptoms. This was not so much due to a modified work environment as to a change in worker expectations towards that environment. As a result, productivity in same cases declined. ·

Having experienced difficulties, managements began to take remedial measures. Improvements could be made in many areas, especially in work environment and conditions of work. Upon closer examination, a number of managements concluded that one of the most promising areas was work itself. This decision was also much in line with some of the latest theories and experiences. Thus, the new area of management focus came into existence as the quality of working life.

In India, context the QWL as a movement may be cousidered rising but, the concept is viewed in terms of western and context, where there are wide variations in Indian and western culture. The set of industrial norms are quite different in both the civilizations and on top of this as compared to west, Indian's industrial growth is in developing stage. In India, inspite of efforts by the Government and the private sector, the unorganised sector is still existing which is as vast as the organised sector.

In india the concept of QWL is considered useful to improve working conditions only for higher level workers. Perhaps no significant attempt has been made to explore

QWL of the workers at the lower level and specially, unorganized sector has remained untouched. This does not mean that workers in the unorganised sector do not have any perception of their life in the context of their work.

Some of the objective parametres have been studied and a little glance has been made by some of the labour market studies to curb the malpractices of bonded labour in India which does not seem to be totally eradicated but their status surveys have thrown light on their conditions of work.

After studying the QWL movement and interest of many social and behavioural scientist in it, it was realised that the concept should be applied for indepth study of workers in the unorganised sector of industries.

Women are the most downtrodden in the world of work, over burdened with hard and arduous work in dual role playing situation, at place of work as well as at home while performing economic responsibility and domestic discourses. Women workers in the construction industry are being considered the lowest in the ladder of workers.

Quality of Working Life : Concept and terms

The notion of quality of working life, as an English idiom is closely related to the quality of life concept. Both emerged relatively recently in the industrialised nations where English was the primary language. Parallel concepts and innovative moves towards life goals developed, however, almost simultaneously in several other industrial countries. Humanisation of work, for instance, is often used in a number of languages as a synonym for quality of working life. In France and other French speaking countries, the most usual expression is "improvement of working conditions", while in the socialist countries the established term is "workers protection". In Scandinavia, the central concepts are "working environment" and "democratisation of the work place". However, the English concept of "quality of working life" is broadly understood in all industrialised countries, even if it is sometimes barely used (Thorsrud, 1976). In the case of Japan, for instance, the concepts of *hatarakiqai* and *ikiqui* which gained impetus in usage around the same time, are surprisingly similar to those of quality of working life and quality of life respectively. These developments would appear to indicate that the majority of industrialised nations have undergone certain common experience during the past quarter of a century.

Sayeed and Sinha (1981) stated that from the time of Taylor (1911) researchers have over the years, dwelt upon the development of working conditions and other related aspects, falling within the realm of social sciences. Most of the work in the area of industrial and organizational psychology had one common feature or an ulterior goal, primarily aimed at improving quality of work and working life and enhancing employee motivation in order to increase organizational viability.

A variety of concepts have been used to map up the conditions of QWL. Earlier, it was called morale and later termed as human relations, organizational development and redesign of work system. Presently, many researchers are inclined to describe the industrial democracy as a measure of quality of working life. Whatever way we have attempted to understand it, the question still remains whether we have made any headway in this direction in terms of integrating relevant findings to result in a new area of enquiry?

Attempts at defining the concept of QWL has been made by many. Taylor's (1973) and Sprin's (1975) view point can be considered for an operational definition which describes QWL as "the degree of excellence in work and working conditions which contribute to the overall satisfaction of the individual and enhances individual as well as organizational effectiveness." Prominent among those who have contributed to the area are Herrick and Maccoby (1972), Heizel, Geodale, Jayner and Burke (1973), Cherns (1973, 1975), Davis and Cherns (1975), Emery and Thorsrud (1976), Macy and Mervis (1976), Graen, Cashman, Ginsburg and Schiemann (1977) and Miller (1977).

The work on QWL had begun in India a decade ago with differences in the social, cultural, political and economic spheres. A major thrust in this area was a tough proposition. But social scientists have gradually weaned their way and the efforts of Ganguly (1976), Joseph (1978) De (1977, 1980), Mehta (1976) and Sinha (1977) are to be lauded. It is further interesting to note that most of the work in the Indian setting dealt with the QWL in a theoretical and descriptive framework or mostly in an action research context to bring about some desirable changes in the design of work system (De, 1980).

The psychological factors have been seen from the angle of labour problems by Delamotte and Takezawa (1974) in their report for International Labour Organization on QWL. They defined QWL as a set of new labour problems and their counter measures which have quined recognition as important determinants of worker satisfaction and productivity in many societies during the period of their sustained economic growth.

Sashkin and Lengermann (1984) have taken a thread from Herzburg's two-factor theory and considered 'conditions' (C) and 'feeling' (F) towards these conditions as important determinants of QWL.

The QWL—C/F is the result of a ten-year research programme that is based on classical sociological analysis of the relation between work and workers in society. These approaches suggest that workers become alienated from their work when the work has little inherent meaning such as repetition of the same minute set of actions over and over or denies the worker control or power over his or her own actions. These conditions lead to subjective feelings of alienation that sociologists call "self-estrangement"—feelings of being cut off from one's own true working self (Blauner, 1964).

In 1970, several research projects were initiated to empirically examine the relations between alienating job conditions which we now refer to as "quality of work life conditions" and workers' self-estrangement which we call 'quality of work life feelings'. These working results led to a series of studies involving computer operators, clerical workers, machine operators, and medical technologists (Kirsch and Lengermann, 1971; Maurer, 1972). This work continue in order to explore effects over time, however, the instrument that was developed during the process of research now has enough evidences of validity to be generally useful (Wilmoph, 1983).

Measurement of QWL

In view of the dearth of systematic work in the area of quality of working life, the measurement of the same seemed to be a practical difficulty. Majority of the studies in this area are theoretically oriented, concerned with what QWL is or what are its dimensions that should be included in the measurement of QWL. Though the list of QWL dimensions to be considered for its measurement is quite exhuastive, with the exceptions of General Motor's Survey (as reported by Carlson, 1978). The QWL dimensions mentioned by other investigators are either speculative or arbitrarily selected. Apart from this most of the surveys have been conducted in the western countries.

Boisvert (1977) identified fifteen dimensions for measuring the QWL. On the other hand, Walker's (1975) quality of working life involved the task, the physical work environment and the social environment within the organisation, the administrative system of the enterprise and the relationship between life and the job. Similarly, Ghosh and Kalra (1982), Ganguli (1979), Joseph (1978), Carlson (1977) etc. took different dimensions for their study of quality of working life. The important of all these studies are by Carlson and Walton in American set-up and Sinha and Syeed in Indian set-up. Very little, however, has been done at the empirical level to relate QWL dimensions with various processes of the organization.

Sashkin and Lengermann (1984) have taken a combination of two factors i.e. conditions of the work and the feelings aroused and the impression of the worker to each of the condition with emphasis on the productivity in an organization. The conditions of work were measured by autonomy, work speed and routine, task related interaction, personal growth opportunity and work complexity. The feelings have been measured by asking certain questions about various activities of the work.

The dimensions taken by Sayeed and Sinha for the measurement of QWL were, economic benefits, physical working conditions, mental state, career orientation, advancement on merit, job stress, effect on personal life, union-management relations, self-respect, supervisory relations, apathy, confidence in management, meaningful development, control, influence and participation, employee commitment, general life satisfaction and organizational climate.

The studies on QWL have taken various dimensions and at this stage when the concept is in its early stages of development, many more researches need be conducted to exactly identify the dimensions of QWL.

The present investigation also has the same thought to explose various dimensions which are correlated with QWL and also the external factors affecting QWL. The importance of these factors are all the more necessary for the workers of the lowest order.

Changing Technology and QWL

We are living in a period of rapidly increasing wrenching social and technological change. Organization and job structures are undergoing change in response to these developments and because of our increased knowledge of the behaviours of organizations and individuals. Industrial society is in transition from one historical era to another and the environmental characteristics of the emerging era will lead to crisis and marine dislocation, unless there is some form of adaptation. The structures of most purposive organisations based as they are on concepts of the industrial era, are becoming increasingly disfunctional because they stand at the confluence of changes involving technology, social values, economic environment and the practices of management.

The emergence of the post industrial era is stimulated by an ever increasing rate of changes in technology. The latter contributes to changes in values, not only by evoking new social systems and roles for organisational members but by stimulating the rising level of expectations concerning material, social and personal needs. The changes in technology changes the attitudes, aspirations of major segments of society. The seeming ease with which new technology satisfies material needs, coupled with the society's provision of subsistance, lend support for its citizens has stimulated a growing concern on the part of groups and individuals about their relationship to work, its meaningfulness and its values are the concerns of QWL.

The high rate of change of technology has consequences for organization and job structure. On the product side, frequent new developments are leading to the growth of shorter production runs with the resulting need for adaptability of organization and workers to more changes. On the production side, there is the phenomenon of more sophisticated machines and simpler manual activities embeded within automated complex production processes. The advanced technology presents us with a number of opportunities to develop new and more humane organizational forms and jobs leading to a high QWL. First, although it poses new problems, highly sophisticated technology possesses an unrecognised flexibility in relation to social systems. There exists an extensive array of configurations of the technology that within limits can be designed to suit the social systems needs.

The new technology increases the dependence of the organization on individuals and groups and requires more individual commitment and autonomous responsibility in the work place. Their requirements for mutual dependence and independence provide opportunities to redress past deep-seated errors in social organizations and member's roles.

The introduction of technology in the unorganised sectors, specially in the construction industry has affected deployment of heavy equipment for which the workers require basic skills. The training opportunities are limited and if we see gender differences, women are considered out of place. The employment opportunities in agriculture fields are also replacing the women folk as they are unable to handle modern equipments. In this way, the immediate employment to women both in agriculture fields and construction industry are gradually reducing and so is the case with the work force participation rate. This factor would definitely be influencing change in perception of QWL by these workers. All attempts of enhancing the QWL have led to successful results, whatever may be the type of interventions.

Gain from Improved QWL

There are various elements which influence the individual's work experience. Therefore, it is certain that an improved QWL will affect these variables. As the perception of QWL differs from individual to individual so is the gain perceived in various terms. QWL programmes incorporate a number of critical elements including a commitment from top management—acknowledgement from both management and employees that a voluntary desire from both sides to co-operate is essential.

From the organizations, point of view the gain of QWL improvement is significant because there is :

—improved quality,

—increased output,

—reduced absenteeism,

—higher turnover,

—better labour management relation etc. and to employee; the gains are :

—job satisfaction

—greater control over one's own job

—recognition

—increased self esteem

—a sense of accomplishment

—fewer mental health problem, improved physical and psychological health.

In short, we can say that a higher quality of working life can often lead to decreased absenteeism, and higher turn over, few accidents and higher quality and quantity of output of goods and services.

The most direct and immediate gain from an improved QWL is higher job satisfaction. These two phenomenon are so closely related that they are often assumed to be one and the same and people sometimes use it interchangibly. But the term job satisfaction refers to an individual's affective reactions or feelings toward his job and the term QWL refers to the individual work experiences. Job satisfaction is determined largely by how well an individual's actual rewards and experiences on his job are compared to his desired or expected rewards and experiences, it is based largely on job. Quality of work life is a broader concept than job satisfaction in the sense that it includes both the job content and job context.

Generally, the workers having high QWL experience high job satisfaction. Individuals whose important needs are being satisfied by their job related activity, invariably express positive feelings about these jobs and hence, there is increase in individual productivity.

Individual productivity and quality of work life are closely related, specially when productivity is defined in terms of the individual's internal work standards. High productivity is both a cause and an effect of a high quality of work life. The term productivity is much more than merely the quality of the individual's work output. It also includes such work behaviours as poor turnover, absenteeism, defiance of rules and authority, grievances, strikes, union activities, sabotage, theft, accidents and specially the quality of work output. All of these behaviours have been shown to be directly influenced by the individual's job satisfaction, involvement or commitment and these attitudes are directly affected by the quality of the individual's work life. Although, QWL is not the only determinant of individual productivity, yet it is the most important determinant. So, in any attempt to improve productivity the other various factors, both inside and outside the organization, must also be taken into account. A high QWL does not always or necessarily assure a high level of productivity but the poor QWL definitely discourages the productivity to some extent.

Improved quality of working life improves the organisational effectiveness on the whole. If the interests of workers and goals of the organisation are mutually supportive, improvement in the quality of work life will result in gains for both parties. As for example, improvement in job design will produce not only more intrinsically motivating and enriching tasks but also higher individual productivity. However, there are many areas where the interests of individuals are not clear and inevitable conflict with the goals (economic goals) of the organisations that employ them or with the interests of the other groups in the organisation. The worker's demand of more pay or greater security are in direct conflict with the profitability of most organisations and similarly, the demand of increase in power or autonomy of non-management workers because it will cause reduction in autonomy and authority of managers. In these cases significant benefits can be gained from improvement of QWL, which has an impact on the ability of inter-dependent individuals and groups to work together toward organisational goals, to communicate effectively with each other, to co-ordinate their activities and to resolve their conflicts.

The Quality of Women's Working Life

There is fundamental difference in female and male work roles which need extensive examination of the nature of these socially accepted sex-bound roles. Although, no society is a sex based division of labour, there is an extraordinary variety of sex typing of occupations across cultures suggesting that the sex typing is not based on unchangeable, genetic, physiological or psychological differences between the sexes but is and has been a social construct.

The industrialization brought about a revolutionary change in the occupation expansion with varying degree of basic human input required from the workers. This gave impetus to misplacing women socially and in the labour market. The women are still considered inferior to men in terms of skill, pay, prestige and authority.

The female role has to face two conflicting situations in the world of work as responsibility at work place and at home as care taking mother, performing perfect domestic and social activities. This is common for all the societies, irrespective of occupational category.

The quality of working life of women has to undergo various stages in the life cycle. After being prepared to undertake work and coming out of the domestic situation, the marriage brings about numerous changes and extra responsibilities on the part of women workers. At times women have to withdraw themselves from the world of work due to their marriage.

Many studies have proved that like men, women are also motivated to work for money. Working womens' income is of considerable economic importance even when it is additional to the husband's income which determines sufficiency or deprivation in the family.

The QWL of the women workers has so far not been assessed by any of the research study. In India, the efforts were not significant. The need is to undertake indifferent research works to study QWL of women workers.

Earlier Studies on QWL

Since quality of working life is a relatively new concept, most of the work in this area are on a theoretical-descriptive line concerned with how QWL should be defined and measured. However, a few empirical studies have been reported from India which tried to relate QWL to job satisfaction, work performance or managerial expectations or to some demographic variables.

In an attempt to study the relationship between job attitudes and QWL, Joseph (1978) collected data from 96 skilled and semi-skilled technicians in a public sector enterprise, following a questionnaire approach. Conceiving QWL as an evaluation process of one's life in the work context. Job attitudes operationalised in terms of work, pay, promotion, co-workers and supervision. The findings of the study indicated that

(a) attitudes towards the nature of work is clearly associated with QWL. The more one feels that his/her work is interesting, challenging and that it gives him/her a sense of achievement, the higher would be his/her perceived quality of working life;

(b) associates or co-workers have the potential to make QWL high or low, and

(c) attitude towards supervision and pay appear to be least associated with QWL even though supervision seems to be a general factor influencing other job aspects.

Singh and Maggu (1980), while studying the corporate quality of working life, operationalised QWL in terms of five dimensions and collected data from 251 managerial level employees representing 42 organisations. The results showed that QWL was considerably low across all the categories of respondents and across all the parameters of work system, perceived QWL being the poorest in the case of democratisation of work process. It was further observed that the variation in managerial hierarchy, income and experience do not significantly influence the perception of the QWL.

In another study, Ghosh and Kalra (1982) collected the importance ratings of 15 QWL factors from 70 managers in public and private sector organisasions in their attempt to study how the different factors associated with the concept of QWL are influenced by variables like age, income, qualification, experience etc. The results of this study revealed significant perceptual differences only in relation to four factors: employee welfare, advancement based on merit, absence of under job stress and union-management relations. The enquiry further showed that 'employee welfare' was influenced by age and income, 'advancement' based on merit, was influenced by education and experience, absence of under job stress' was influenced by professional, non-professional categories and the perception of 'union-professional categorisation of respondents. However, "various QWL factors are likely to be perceived differently by different groups."

In a more comprehensive study, Sayeed and Sinha (1981) examined the relationship between QWL and job satisfaction and performance taking data from 184 class III employees working in two organizations. For measuring QWL, they used the inventory developed by Sinha and Sayeed (1980). For job satisfaction, they used the same dimensions as used by Joseph for measuring job attitudes. And performance measures were obtained from worker's self and supervisor ratings. Overall, the results indicated that higher QWL leads to greater job satisfaction and better performance.

Emery (1976), Srivastava (1975) and McGregor (1960) in their studies stressed that the organisational structure played a significant role in developing human personality. All these studies have demonstrated beyond doubt that a bureaucratic culture severely inhibits human growth and that it is inadequate for inducing commitment to work, Friedlander and Newton studied the impact of organisational climate on the individual's job values and job satisfaction. They found organisational climate to be a significant determinant of individual job satisfaction. Lyon and Lvaucvich observed that the organisational climate had the most significant impact on self-actualisation a lesser impact on autonomy and only slight impact on esteem.

Inspite of the awareness of these findings and many other researches which clearly high-light the role of the corporate culture and quality of working life in determining human behaviour. Kapoor has concluded that about 25 per cent of the work force is in the dissatisfied range, 30 per cent in the satisfied group and remaining 45 per cent in the neutral zone. In a survey of 2821 American managers, Tarnowieaski concludes that 70 per cent of the managers were satisfied with their present career. The same study reveals that within the preceding five years nearly 50 per cent of the executives surveyed had either changed or seriously considered changing their line of work for more meaningful career. Based on the study of the middle level managers, from 500 organisations Tasrnowieaski further reported that the middle level managers were highly dissatisfied with the contemporary organisational work life.

According to Mehta (1976) work amenities including economic compensation, interpersonal support, autonomy on the job and respectful supervisory behaviours are important factors in work related satisfaction. Studies also suggest the importance of general life satisfaction in promoting work satisfaction and efficient functioning in work organisation (Mehta 1976). Repeated studies done by Mehta (1976) and Veccho (1980) on several categories of people including government officials, managers and supervisory staff show that perceived availability of influence and autonomy are the major source of satisfaction or dissatisfaction. Similarly, influence and autonomy were another important indicators of dissatisfaction at the work place is the employee's perception of lack of amenities such as general welfare amenities and inadequate economic compensation including inadequate salary. In several cases, non-availability of adequate water and canteen facilities, inadequate medicine and health care proved to be a major source of work related dissatisfaction (Mehta, 1976).

In developing countries, various kinds of developmental activities, following political and social freedom have led to very significant rise in the people's aspirations. Such rising aspirations are bound to effect the sense of life satisfaction among the workers. Similarly, socio-economic factors also play an important role in shaping attitudes towards work and related matters in the context of rising aspirations. For instance, studies identified economic factors like income, promotional opportunities, social security as important factors in employee's sense of life satisfaction. Factors like working hours and nature of job did not find same importance as salary, security and advancement (Ganguli 1976).

Another important finding in various studies is related to age of the employees. The young entrants to organisations and younger employees showed greater work related dissatisfaction. Such dissatisfaction tended to decrease with increasing age of the employee (Mehta 1976). Mehta also found that older employees felt more satisfied with life related issues in comparison to the younger ones. Although, it is not clear why the older employees feel so. With the increase in age, they are expected to have greater family and social responsibility and therefore, greater concern for salary increments than younger ones. The dissatisfaction among the younger employees seems to be realistic to a certain extent because they have rising aspirations and expect more from the job than they actually get at the work place.

In another study Ahmed (1971), Ashraf (1975) find that lowly educated younger employees show greater sense of dissatisfaction with their life conditions. As a rule, lesser educated employees also get lower pay and lower benefits as compared to higher educated employees. Dissatisfaction due to economic factors is enhanced by rising aspirations. Such employees carry their dissatisfaction with life conditions with them to their work and work place.

Singh (1982) in his study of quality of corporate work life found that perceived QWL was considerably poor in

Indian industries and perception did not change with the change in the managerial hierarchy. The findings of his study further revealed that the income did not significantly influence the perceived quality of work life.

In another important study, Mehra (1984) found the relationship of job involvement to background factors, perceived importance of needs and need satisfaction. Although, his study was not directly related to individual need fulfilment, yet individual's job involvement has its roots in the principles of need satisfaction and motivation. Job of an individual is of great importance and the individuals involvement in job depends on satisfaction of needs derived by individuals on the job. His study throws light on income and length of service having significant correlation with need fulfilment among other factors. The subjects with more income were found more satisfied with their needs and were more job involved. Level of education and place of birth did not make any difference to the need satisfaction and job involvement.

Livneh (1978) in his study on quality of work experience found that patterns of changes in work values, job reward are contingent on specific facet of work involved, rather than age being uniformly a significant determining factor. He also found that education has the most important relation to various work values followed by occupation.

George (1984) studied lower, middle and upper managerial workers to study QWL in Public Sector Undertakings. Along with the background variables quality of life was correlated with QWL. The results indicated that high quality of life will have high quality of working life, older employees have lower QWL, no relationship existed between length of service and income with QWL.

Mishra (1985) studied quality of working life of managers and Research and Development personnel of two Public Sector Undertakings to find relationship between age, length of service, education, income and need fulfilment. The results indicated that age and length of service did not affect QWL perception. QWL was a function of income of the employees, the high income leads to high QWL, higher the educational level, higher was the QWL perception. QWL was significantly related to need fulfilment.

On the basis of the review of concerned literature and various methods and studies in the direction of concept clarification, following hypotheses were framed for testing. Seven null hypotheses have been framed because the supporting and parallel evidences are not available in the literature surveyed.

Hypothesis I—The difference in the level of QWL will have no relationship with background variables of the women construction workers.

Hypothesis II—The relationship of QWL with work related variables of women workers will not be significant.

Hypothesis III—The living condition variables will not have any significant relation with QWL.

Hypothesis IV—The general awareness of the respondents will have no relation with level of QWL.

Hypothesis V—The attitude towards education of the women construction workers will have no relationship with QWL.

Hypothesis VI—The performance level of the women construction workers will not be significantly related to QWL.

Hypothesis VII—The need fulfilment of the women construction workers will not be significantly related to QWL.

3

Women Workers and Construction Industry

SECTION I

Womens' Roles, Rights and Participation in Economic Activities

The society is intimately connected with its economic position which depends on rights, roles and opportunities in participation of economic activities. The economic position of women is accepted as an indicator of societies stage of development. This does not necessarily mean that all development leads to improving women's economic position. Women's activities are greatly affected by social attitudes and institutions which stem from the social ideology concerning basic components of status in any given period.

The economic role of women and the need for equality of rights and opportunities of economic participaticn has three basic arguments :

(a) women's economic subjugation or dependent position is the result of a rigid distinction in man's and woman's role in society which leads to exploitation;

(b) the full benefit of development can only be realized with peoples' participation i.e. effective use of human resources and the economic role of women which cannot be isolated from the total framework of development;

(c) socio-economic and political change creates a need to extend spheres of knowledge and activity of all members of a society. Modern trends in demographic and social changes call for a redefinition of women's role in family and society, changes in age of marriage, family size, urbanization, migration, rising costs and standard of living call for greater participation in decision making process in family as well as in the society. These roles have to be recognized, enabling women to meet these challenges by removal of social handicaps and obstacles.

Apart from these, women's roles have now acquired greater importance in the world of technological advancement. The biasness of considering women as mentally and physically handicap in handling of technological equipments has to be removed by creating equal opportunities of learning new types of skills. Mahatma Gandhi pointed out that :

> "Today the sole occupation of the women against us is supposed to be bearing children, looking after her husband and otherwise to drudge for the household··· not only is the women condemned to domestic slavery, but when she goes out as a labourer to earn wages, though she works harder than man she is paid less."

Similar observations were made by a number of other authors. Some of the research studies support that in world of work, women contribute much more than men. Mead (1975) found little physical determination in performing of role and traced important characteristics of women in one culture which were those of men in the other. Today, it is an approved fact that two-third of world's work is performed by women, yet the women are rated with an ignorable status of 'non-workers' and play a marginal role in socio-economic participation. For ages they have been considered as a 'weaker sex', their share in world's property is at no more than one per cent. In developing world and in the developed countries also women do not share the resources and rewards of the economic development equally with man.

It is not difficult to trace out of the genesis of grand exploitative mechanism, thrusting domestic work upon women as their exclusive domain. With the help of what Commer (1974) terms, "odd mixture of sentimentality, dobious logic and straight forward prejudices" like Arab and the Camel episode, women have been led from domestic work to domestication of work under subjugation of men as slaves. The domestic work as Rogers (1979) aptly observes, is essential to social and economic structure of which the family is a basic unit, at the same time, it is petty, isolated, monotonous and requires virtually unending hours of work. Much of it is hard and unrewarding. It requires intensive labour, still it is unpaid. It is readily believed that women do not work as long as they do full time house work.

There is a vicious circle which perpetuates and even accelerates this explotive situation. Various socio-economic, religious, cultural, psychological barriers confine women to a state, deterrent to their development. Social prestige is accorded to their "non-working status" and stigma is attached to their working status. In all circumstances, the demand and supply factor of human resources discriminate and push women to the bottom of work hierarchy. It was, therefore, Lenin felt compelled to describe that :

> "Home work is the most unproductive, the most barbarous and the most arduous work a woman can do. It is exceptionally petty and does not include anything that would in any way promote the development of the woman."

Modernisation has further helped in exploitation of women. The process of modernisation has followed a pattern, creating dual economy. One with capital intensive modern sector and the other with labour intensive traditional stereotyped colony, giving birth to "Internal Colonialism". In the domestic as well as the export oriented modern sector, women with lower level skills or no skills are exploited in their wage payments for monotonous and strainuous work. The supervisory or excutive positions are enjoyed by men. The male bias in work and development perpetuates. Planners and policy makers generally remain insensitive to the position of women within the patriarchical power-structure in the family and unequal power relation between women and men in the community. In the domestic structure of inequality, women are underdeveloped and continue to remain underdeveloped in comparison to men.

Household work or domestic work remains unaccounted for in National Domestic Product statistics. According to Mitra (1981) the participation of women in India, in other informal sectors, varied from 41 to 49 per cent as against 15 to 17 per cent in the case of men. Women frequently have to assume the role of principal bread winners in addition to their other responsibilities. It may be necessary to redefine the indices of national income and assign appropriate value to domestic or non-market work. "Home production activities, as observed by Srinivasan (1974), mainly include food processing and meal preparation, care and maintenance of household. These activities are now considered as contribution to real income and consumption of this income in the household."

Women are exploited. They are made to accept highly labour intensive monotonous and arduous work. Women put more hours of work than men and the earnings of men are invested mostly on menfolk on the terms of better food, clothing, health, education, leisure and recreation. Women are forced to have subsistence living. The surpluses are enjoyed by men for their further betterment. This vicious circle operates to worsen the development of women and to confine the prospects of betterment to males alone.

Attempts have also been made to define economic and gainful work. Raj (1976) defines gainful/productive/economic work as "work contributing to income generation or gain of some kind." The time spent in productive work is that which involved efforts and produce some utilities. Similarly, Farouk (1975) defines "productive work" as to include all income generation activities, expenditure saving activities at home and also the manifold household chores. He finds that rural women spend about 12 to 14 hours daily in productive work as against 10 to 11 productive hours by men. ILO study (1977) reveals that "in the rural areas... women are over-worked. They are responsible for much of the work in agricultural production as well as for virtually all food preparation and the care of children." Chakravarty (1975) finds that women in Haryana work for 15 to 16.5 hours a day.

It is equally necessary to build a new social infrastructure with non-exploittaive values of equality and development. From the view point of improving the demand for women labour, it is crucial that all social, cultural and attitudinal prejudices against their employment are removed but gradual improvement of QWL with careful implementation may bring about changes in perception of society towards women. Women must be given education, training in new skills and technology for taking up progressive occupations and constantly improving and reimproving their quality of work life.

Women Employment Trends in Economic Participation—an Indicator of QWL

Employment refers to performance of work for earning. One of the crude indicators of women's participation in employment as well as development is a study of labour force/work force participation ratios. The statistics of participation rates, however, need to be studied with caution in order to know some indicators of QWL of women. Higher participation rate does not necessarily indicate "better off" state of affairs Low productivity, poverty and high participation may go together.

There are three major sources of data on employment and unemployment: the census, various rounds of National

Sample Survey and the Employment Market Information Programme of Directorate General of Employment and Training. Census data is limited because of conceptual difference in the definition of workers. The National Sample Survey apart from the smaller size of the sample and shorter reference periods, do nottake into consideration the sharp seasonal variations in the labour force participational rates. The data on women workers from these two sources also form reporting bias, particularly for the large unorganised sector of the economy where the majority of women are employed and do not permit an evaluation of the total women labour potential and its relevant characteristics. A sizeable proportion of labour input in household enterprises is provided by family workers who have only partial attachment to the labour market. While their *inclusion in labour force* would be misleading. Their total exclusion would also fail to reflect reality of their economic situation.

The Employment Market Information Programme covers all public and private sector establishments which employ 10 or more workers, excluding all self-employed persons and unpaid family workers engaged in small non-agricultural establishments, agriculture, small plantations and private construction activities. These estimates are useful only for assessing the employment situation in the urban organised sector.

1981 Census defined workers as one who participates in any economically productive activity. Such participation may be physical or mental in nature, 'involving' not only actual work but also effective supervision and directions to work. The definition does not include other parametres of QWL.

A number of empirical studies reveal that in the past, the development has not necessarily increased the labour force participation rates. It has rather pushed down the participation ratios both for women and men due to various reasons and one of them may be due to lack of improvements in QWL.

With increased income the desire for more leisure and loss of work tends to get stronger and thus, it adversely effects participation ratio, until new consumerism again pulls up the demand for income and work. This is a plausible explanation for the world-wide falling number in working hours and declining trend in work force participation ratio during the current century which perhaps brought about consciousness of QWL. It has been recently experienced in Kerala where with the increased inflow of income from the Arab countries, the females have started withdrawing from the work participation. During 1971-81 Kerala recorded declining trend in the female participation rates.

There is another aspect of falling work-force participation rates with development. The decrease in overall level of activity rates, associated with modern economic development in fact, does not signify that "fewer persons enter the labour force during their life-time but that the years of their participation are shortened by later entry into labour force and earlier retirement" (Farooq, 1967).

The entry to job gets delayed as the modern work requirements entail more of initial education and skill development. Similarly, in the later years requiring renewed training and education may force people to seek early retirement. The changing sophistications in techniques of production may result in decrease in the propensity to take advantage of various job opportunities in the old age.

The studies related to female work participation reveal that the impact of development is more adverse on their participation than for the males as the overall decline in the participation rates during the last century has been much steeper in case of female than male. There are a number of studies which indicate that development has often supressed females to peripheral and stagnant employments which provide, at best, horizontal mobility. This factor affect perception of QWL by women.

Age-specific female labour force participation rates all over the wor'd present mossic picture. For developed western block (market economics), it is somewhat rising from the age of 20 years, reaching at peak at the age of 24-25 years and recording steep decline upto 30-35 years and again rising thereafter until the age of 40-45 years and again start falling after the age of 60 years or so. In the developing countries like India the age specific female participation curve record the peak at the age of 31-44 years and it continues to rise from the age of 5 to 44 years. The high participation rate of females in the age group of 15-44 years is responsible for alarmingly high mortality rates of the women in the age group.

Table 3.1

Labour Force Participation Rates by Age Group and Sex 1977-78 in India

Age Group (years)	*Rural*		*Urban*	
	Male	*Female*	*Male*	*Female*
5-14	14.60	11.90	6.44	4.66
15-29	87.89	51.45	74.54	25.67
30-44	99.10	61.87	98.96	32.41
45-59	96.34	53.76	93.93	29.12
60 and above	66.76	22.06	51.75	12.97
All 5 and more	64.69	39.27	60.75	20.33

Source : GOI, NSS 32 Round.

In the western developed market economies, the disparity in male and female participation rates continue to persist. However, some converging trend in this regard is perceptible during the last three decades. In India the disparity in male and female work force participation rates during the current century has changed erratically as evident from the Table 3.2.

Table 3.2

States and Union Territories Arranged in Descending Order of their 1981 Female Work Participation Rates

Female Participation Rank in 1981 State/U.T.	*Work Participation Rates*			
	1981		*1971*	
	Female	*Male*	*Female*	*Male*
1	*2*	*3*	*4*	*5*
1. Nagaland	40.83	50.09	45.24	55.55
2. Arunachal Pradesh	40.64	56.63	51.28	63.14
3. Manipur	36.52	46.69	23.62	45.31
4. Meghalaya	34.97	53.62	34 57	53.21
5. Sikkim	34.68	56.23	41.85	62.96
6. Mizoram	32.73	49.14	39.46	51.43
7. Andhra Pradesh	27.87	56.16	24.16	58.22
8. Dadra and Nagar Haveli	26.20	55.11	38.96	55.43
9. Maharashtra	24.39	53.14	19.70	59.09
10. Madhya Pradesh	22.63	52.43	18.65	53.74
11. Tamil Nadu	22.57	55.36	15.09	56.02
12. Karnataka	19.23	53.75	14.20	54.40
13. Himachal Pradesh	18.80	48.81	29.79	52.43
14. Goa, Daman and Diu	15.10	45.86	15.40	47.67
15. Kerala	12.79	40.77	13.49	45.00
16. Gujarat	11.85	51.77	10.26	51.24
17. Pondicherry	11.05	45.90	10.94	48.65
18. Orissa	10.88	54.38	6.81	55.32
19. Rajasthan	9.44	49.65	8.34	52.09
20. Bihar	9.16	49.08	8.88	52.16
21. Tripura	9.08	49.06	4.83	49.43
22. Chandigarh	8.87	54.17	5.70	53.96
23. Delhi	6.39	50.57	4.75	50.61

1	*2*	*3*	*4*	*5*
24. Uttar Pradesh	6.02	49.61	6.71	52 24
25. West Bengal	5.97	48.97	4.43	48.83
26. Andaman and Nicobar Islands	5.03	54.22	4 53	62.10
27. Haryana	4.82	48.17	2.53	47.27
28. Punjab	3.09	52.01	1.18	52.82
India	14.44	51.23	12.13	52.61

Source : Census of India 1981.

Disparities in Work Force Participation Affecting QWL

The incidence of relative sex disparity ratio (DR) in work force participation rate can be measured as ratio between male participation rates (MPR) and female participation rate (FPR). This may be shown by simple mathematical expression as follows :

$$DR = \frac{MPR}{FPR}$$

It is revealing to note that the disparities between male and female work participation rates during the past eight decades in India have been continuously increasing (excepting during 1971-81). It may be seen that during 1901-1981 the disparity of women in work force vis-a-vis males, increased from 1.9 times in 1901 to 3.5 times in 1981, reaching at peak in 1971 when the dispartity ratio was of the order of 4.3 times. The National Sample Survey (NSS) data available for the last three decades for rural and urban areas also shows similar results.

Table 3.3

Worker Population Ratio by Sex in NSS Rounds (1960-61—1977-78) and Censuses

NSS Round No. and Reference Period		*Status of Employment*		*Participation*	
		Rural		*Urban*	
		Male	*Female*	*Male*	*Female*
(16) July 1960-June 1961	One week	54.2	25.9	52.3	1
(20) July 1966-June 1967	One week	53.0	27.3	50.6	1
(27) Oct. 1972-Sept. 1973	Usual Status	54.3	32.5	50.1	1
(31) July 1977-June 1978	—do—	53.0	24.5	49.5	1
		Censuses			
1961	Usual Status	58.3	31.42	52.1	1
1971	—do—	53.8	15.8	48.9	1
1981	—do—	54.3	23.9	49.7	1

Source : NSS and Census Reports.

The female participation rate as reported in Censuses is usually low and there are some possibilities of under enumeration on account of socio-cultural stigma subjecting people to under report female employment. Infact, the female labour force measurement and analysis suffer from what Jain (1982) sums up "under enumeration, inadequate attention to unpaid female labour, home production and household work and the relationships between these. There are poor conceptualisation of female work styles, mistaken perception of female economic roles by respondents and interviewers." These aspects need indepth study in the context of QWL.

Intra-rural and intra-unban disparities in male and female age specific work force participation rates urban disparities in male and female age-specific work force participation rates in India are rather alarming.

Table 3.4

Work Force Participation Rates by Sex and Age Groups in Rural and Urban in 1971

Age Groups (in year)	*Rural*		*Urban*		*Total*	
	M	*F*	*M*	*F*	*M*	*F*
0-14	7.52	2.96	—	—	6.63	2.56
15-19	62.09	18.39	33.12	5.47	55.24	15.49
20-24	86.31	20.20	67.44	9.50	81.30	17.85
25-29	95.33	21.78	90.53	11.63	94.19	19.93
30-39	97.56	23.44	95.45	13.05	97.09	21.44
40-49	97.58	24.12	95.16	14.47	97.06	22.38
50-59	95.46	20.78	87.89	12.66	94.02	19.40
60 and above	77.42	11.31	55.36	6.42	73.79	10.49
Age not stated	29.51	5.86	52 36	7.62	33.96	6.05
Total	53.46	13 09	6.61	48.82	52.05	11.85

Source : Census of India—1971.

Table 3.5

Trend in Work Force Participation Rates 1901-1981

Year	*Male*	*Female*	*Disparity Index*	*Terms Used for "Economically Active"*
1901	62.1 (73,864)	31.7 (37,249)	1.9	"Actual worker"
1911	61.9 (79,000)	33.7 (41,360)	1.8	—do—
1921	60.5 (77,220)	32.7 (39,830)	1.8	—do—
1931	60.5 (82,480)	27.6 (36,000)	2.1	"Earner"
1951	54.0 (98,930)	23.3 (40,370)	2.3	"Self supporting and earning dependent"
1961	57.1 (124,946)	27.9 (57,596)	2.0	"Worker"
1971	52.6 (144,089)	12.1 (30,943)	3.0	"Main activity workers plus non-worker having secondary work"
1981	51.2 (174,115)	14.4 (45,967)	3.5	"Actual productive work"

Figures in brackets represent total worker (in '000).

Source : (i) Census of India Reports.

(ii) K.C. Seal : "Women in the Labour Force in India. India : A Macro Land Statistical Profile" Women in the Labour Force (ARTEP) : As an Employment Programmes, ILO, Bangkok, p. 24.

In urban areas this disparity is much more than rural areas. The magnitude of disparity is nearly eight times in urban areas as against four times in rural areas. In the developed market economies, the differences in male female age-specific labour force participation rates are less pronounced and these are simply marginal in socialist group of countries.

Women in the Unorganised Sector—Objective Indicators of QWL

94 per cent of the women workers are engaged in unorganised sector of the economy, 84 per cent in agriculture and

rest in other non-agricultural occupations. Many of the women agriculture labour have to migrate in search of employment to other non-agricultural occupations in the unorganised sectors. They are outside the reach of most laws and the absence of labour organisations. Wherever they exist, they are still in formative stages and have had little impact on women. The female workers in India largely belong to economically weaker sections of the society, in highly arduous occupations as agricultural labours, construction worker, mining and quarring, domestic servants, vendors, etc. without any benefit of social security and other privileges. The female work among this constitutes "distressed sale" of their labour which can hardly be supported upon moral and ethical grounds.

The women workers in the unorganised sector suffer due to lack of education and about 33 per cent are illiterates and about 13.5 per cent are educated upto middle level. This labour force do not have much of skill for the type of occupation they hold which may in due course, lead to low productivity at exploitated situations in the labour market.

The gradual commercialization and modernization of economy have further worsen the situation for this category of labour force. The traditional roles of women are so rigid that they have been considered incapable of modern technique and in this process having thrown out of the labour market.

The number of women in construction industry has increased from 2.9 lakhs in 1951 to 5.37 lakhs in 1981. The Government is the largest employer as public constructions such as dams, bridges, roads and public buildings which make up the major share of expenditure in this industry. The Committee on Status of Women (1975) initiated two studies on women construction workers, one in Patna (covering 3 major projects), and the other in Delhi (covering 9 construction sites). Findings of these studies illustrate the conditions of women in the industry.

Ph.-1 Womens' work is arduous.

Ph.-2 Insecurity and instability of employment

Women are employed mostly as unskilled labourers for carrying earth, mortar or bricks, crushing bricks and working on hand-pumps. Recruitment is mostly done either directly by the contractor or the sub-contractor (Jamadar). Wage payment is on daily or weekly basis. The Bihar Study reported that the sub-contractors obtain a contract for the job on piece but pay their workers on daily basis, ensuring a higher margin of profit for themselves. Workers complain of short payment and unexplained deductions. The system of deferred wage payment and unjustified fines and deductions are reported in both the studies. The Delhi group reported that apart from fines, the Jamadar deducted 25-50 paise per day from their wages without giving any reasons. The existence of these intermediaries invariably depresses the wage rates. Women from all the three Bihar projects reported wage differentials between men and women. In Delhi, such a distinction has been abolished since 1961.

The household incomes of nearly 80 per cent of respondents in Delhi study was between Rs. 200 and Rs.300. The per-capita monthly income was below Rs. 75 for 45 per cent and below Rs. 50 for a little over 20 per cent. For the Bihar study the average household income ranged from Rs. 194 to Rs. 334. Per capita monthly income ranges from Rs. 39 to Rs. 67. For all the families covered by these two studies, the earnings of the women constitute the major share of the families income. The expenditure pattern reported by both the studies indicated that the major part of income was spent on food and other essential items of daily need, 37 per cent of the Delhi study and 37.7 per cent of the Bihar study (58.7 per cent among non-tribals and 10.3 per cent among tribals) were in debt. The most important reasons for taking loans were sickness, to meet gaps in normal consumption and marriage expenses. These debts generally remain unpaid.

These women are mostly drawn from the rural poor (77.6 per cent of the Bihar study and 86 per cent of the Delhi study). The Delhi study consists of migrant labour from Rajasthan and out of 150 respondents 144 belong to the

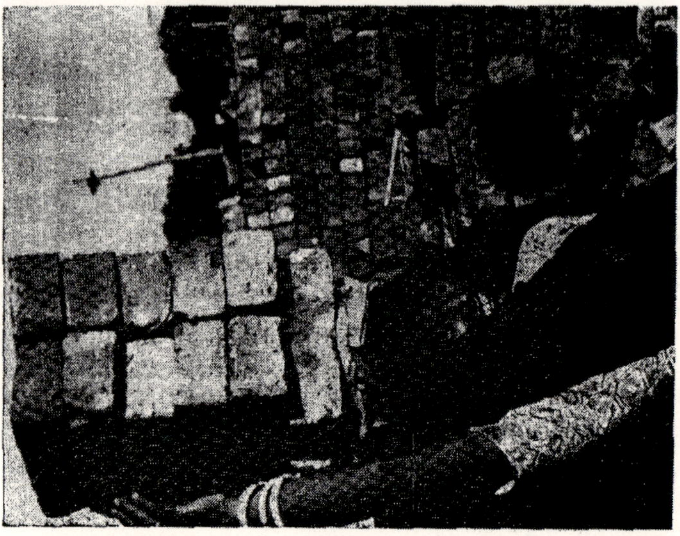

Ph.-4 The dual role conflict.

Ph.-3 Immediate employment.

scheduled caste. 90 per cent respondents of the Bihar study belong to the scheduled castes and scheduled tribes from the Chhota Nagpur region. Almost all the respondents reported poverty as their main reason for taking up construction work. One interesting feature reported in the Delhi study is that in 40 per cent cases the decision was taken by the women themselves while in 60 per cent of the women respondents were persuaded by their husbands and relatives. 78 per cent of the Bihar and 81 per cent of the Delhi study were young women below 35 years as the nature of construction work makes heavy demands on physical strength. 40 per cent of Delhi study respondents become employed before reaching their 15th year and 40 per cent had already worked for more than 7 years. At least 1/5th of them had worked for more than 4 jobs. Of the Bihar study, 81 per cent women had begun their working life as wage labourers very easily in their childhood. Of the rest 12.7 per cent became wage labourers between the ages of 15-20 years. The age composition of the women shows that the Bihar study 8.7 per cent women were below 15, 47.3 per cent between 15-25, 28 per cent were between 25-35 and 22 per cent were over 35 years of age. Of the Delhi study 40 per cent women were between 15-25, 40.6 per cent were between 25-35 and 19.3 per cent were over 35 years of age.

98 per cent of all women respondents were illiterate. Of the Delhi study more than 90 per cent were married before the age of 15 years. As many as 43 per cent were married before the age of 10. Of the Bihar study 12.9 per cent were married before the age of 10, 37.6 per cent were married between 10 to 15 and 32 per cent between 15-20. The majority of this last group were tribal women, since the average age of marriages of the tribal group was 18.4 while that of the non-tribal women was 11.4. 11.3 per cent women of the Bihar study were widows or deserted wives.

About 23 per cent women of the Delhi study had continued working till the last day during pergnancy and 40 per cent till the 8th or 9th month. This indicated that the provisions of the Contract Labour Act guaranteeing maternity

Ph.-5 Lack of skill development opportunities

Ph.-6 Misfits of industrial modernisation.

leave have not been enforced in case of these women. Absence of the minimumhealth protection during pregnancy as well as continuous mal-nutrition has resulted in high infant mortality, 645 children had been born during the project period to these women but at the time of the survey only 389 of them were alive. For the Bihar study out of 233 children born to these women, 67 died. 29 of these died before reaching the age of one year. A comparison of the tribal and non-tribal groups showed that the average number of births and deaths was nearly double amongst the non-tribal women than amongst the tribals. The Bihar study also reveals that the majority of the women continued working even when they were ill rather than go without good for themselves and their dependents.

Under the rules of the Central Public Works Department, contractors are bound to provide fair wages and welfare services like creches, housing of specific standard and sanitary services. Working hours, weekly day for rest, over time rates, wage periods and rates payment and the name of inspecting officer are to be notified by the Department. The inspecting officer is responsible for enforcement of these rules and has to investigate cases of complaint or disputes under the Industrial Dispute and Workmen's Compensation Act. The Bihar Government has also made regulations for controlling the terms and conditions of employment of the labour force employed by the contractors. But it appears that most of these regulations are not honoured in the breach than in compliance. Though the survey did not attempt to find out the reasons for the non-implementation of these regulations, it is not difficult to form the observation that no serious attempt was made by the Government authorities to see that these regulations were enforced. The Bihar study which covered only Government projects reported that the period of actual work was found invariably exceeding the scheduled 48 hours per week. On particular days the period exceeded the maximum of 9 hours by 4 and 5 hours. None of them received pay for the weekly holidays. Though overtime was common, payment for such work was rare, primarily because of the ignorance of the workers and the absence of the law enforcing agency. No arrangements had been made for creches in any of the three sites, though many of the respondents were carrying small children with them to work.

The Delhi study reported that though in most cases women earned as much as their husbands, they did not enjoy equality of status within the family. Only about 8 per cent of the women said that they had a say in taking decisions in respect of matters like daily expenditure, education and marriage of children and selection of jobs. The rest of the respondents stated that the decisions were taken by their husbands or by the parent-in-laws.

Mobile creches—a voluntary organization, conducted a census survey of their 28 centres in Delhi in 1979 and reported that these centres were located in urban resettlement colonies and on construction sites. Of the 47 per cent, on whom data were available, 23 percent subjects were from low castes, 15 per cent from medium castes, and 9 per cent from high castes.

61.3 per cent of mothers belonged to the age group of 21-30 years, 30 per cent in the age range of 31-40 years. 2.7 per cent in 41-50 years. 90.4 per cent of the mothers from construction sites were illiterate. 69 per cent working mothers on construction sites earned approximately Rs. 180 per month.

94 per cent of the fathers were employed and a small number i.e. 23 per cent were unemployed. On the construction sites, 1.2 per cent fathers were employed as skilled workers, 46 per cent as labourers.

Only a small number of families had a few other sources of income. These were mainly the contribution of another member of the family earning or from some small trade. The majority of the sample (80.7 per cent) had no income from outside what they earned in their regular jobs. 92.5 per cent of the families were nuclear in structure and the rest were joint.

89 per cent of the children lived with both parents. The majority of the parents from the construction sites (71.8 per

cent) had stayed in Delhi for less than five years and only 14.1 per cent had been in Delhi for more than 11 years.

National Buildings Organisation sponsored five studies (1977-78) in Delhi, Ahmedabad, Poona, Madras, KALVAL (Kanpur, Agra, Varanasi, Lucknow and Allahabad) and surveyed 3425 workers for the assessment of working and living conditions. The results indicated that there is a constant problem of instability of employment for the workers. The recruitment system was generally through Jamadars and employment exchange has insignificant roles in job seeking. The migration of the workers was because of unemployment at home, insufficient income and indebtedness, expectation of better prospects in the city was found as the main reason of migration to city. 96 per cent workers in Delhi, 69 per cent in Ahmedabad, 78 per cent in Poona, 70 per cent in Madras and 59 per cent in KALVAL towns were migrants from rural or other urban areas.

The building construction industry is predominantly a male dominated economic activity due to the arduous nature of work to be performed by the workers.

The proportion of women workers was 5.2 per cent in Delhi, 25.5 per cent in Ahmedabad, 19.8 per cent in Poona, 25.4 per cent in Madras and 2.3 per cent in KALVAL towns, and almost all of them were employed on unskilled jobs. The women workers generally remain unskilled inspite of their continuous employment in construction for a number of years. The contractors also find the employment of women workers beneficial because they perform the same type of task as men and are sometimes paid wages at lesser rate.

The earnings of the construction workers fluctuate on account of discontinuity of employment which generally occur due to rains, non-availability of building materials and change of sites. 90 per cent of the skilled workers were getting more than Rs. 200 per month whereas the unskilled were getting less. The workers are generally illiterates but those who are

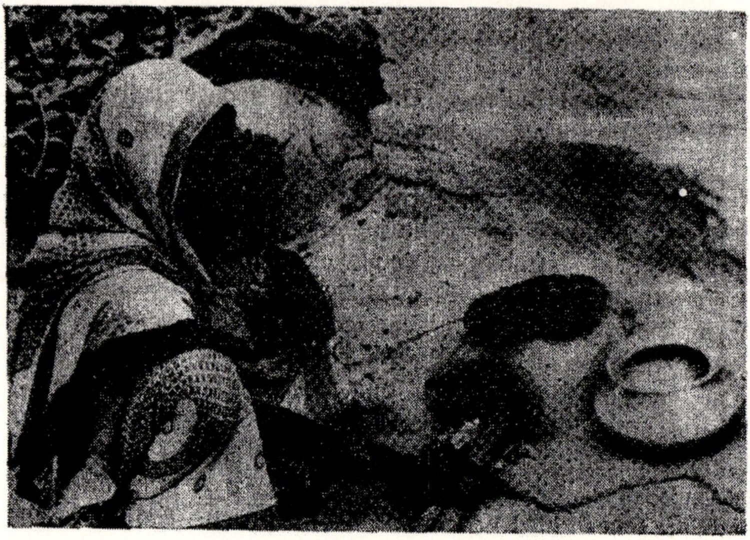

Ph.-7 Household responsibilities.

Ph.-8 Sub standard housing facility.

literates, were of very low level. Literacy level among women was almost negligible.

Employment relationship in the construction industry was determined by a simultaneous interaction of a set of socio-economic variable with contextual factors. The discontinued *nature of employment prevents a direct and continued relation* with employers. Thereby, inhibiting the growth of uniform and collective bargaining in the labour marketing process.

The working conditions of the workers were found extremely unsatisfactory inspite of properly framed laws, implementation of these were almost absent.

The study of Madras reveals that uncertainty of work and low wages were the reasons of dissatisfaction. Only 42 per cent of the respondents expressed desire to continue working in the construction industry.

In Ahmedabad the average monthly income of the workers was only Rs. 195. The study estimated that 78 per cent of the households were poor and living below the poverty line. The same study revealed that the labour productivity in building construction is relatively higher in comparison to large scale manufacturing sector.

All these studies indicate that the removal of insecurity feelings by providing stabilisation of employment could be brought about and improvement in quality of working life would release raising productivity levels. Infact, basic dimensions of quality of working life are not available in this industry to the workers.

SECTION II

Salient Features of Construction Industry

Development Goals

The major goals of development in developing countries are to raise quality of life of the poorest section of the society to a minimum standard. This objective has been given special attention in so far prepared Seven Five Year Development Plans. The early plans envisaged rapid rate of growth of the national product as the base of the establishment of a prosperous society. This approach ensured limited available resources and channelised them into the most productive lines to generate enough surplus for saving and reinvestment. Capital accumulation was thus, considered the sole means of economic growth. It was presumed that once the growth takes place, it will automatically spread its effect and activise various sectors and create employment opportunities for the people, leading to an overall improvement in quality of life and welfare of the masses.

Various studies have shown that satisfactory rate of growth by itself does not lead to amelioration of poverty. The growth has not always been able to make significant impact on employment and poverty. On the contrary, unemployment and inequalities in all spheres of life accentuated.

Current thinking has therefore, remarkably changed the approach to development planning. A high growth rate is necessary but not sufficient condition to ensure employment generation and income distribution in favour of the masses to reduce poverty. The growth has to be linked with ultimate goal of planning and in doing so, the aspect of income distribution in the growth process cannot be divorced from the production aspect. It is, therefore, increasingly being realised that new development strategies must be aimed at for the satisfaction of the basic human needs rather than at fulfilling the market demand.

In India, economic growth has been accompanied by a rapid expansion of educational system growing literacy, improvement in nutrition, health conditions, increasing technological sophistication and structural changes, including a growing industrial base and greater urbanisation. Despite these achievements much remains to be accomplished.

Past experience has given rise to a broad consensus about the goals for future. Development efforts are not directed towards the objectives of (i) rapid growth, (ii) fuller employment, (iii) distributive justice, and (iv) fulfilment of basic human needs of the masses in general and of the poor sections in particular. Most developing countries are designing their developmental strategies to realise these objectives. In doing so, the process of growth in all these countries will have to be restructured to ensure a wider diffusion of income and employment and measures undertaken be a direct attack on the problem of poverty.

Rapid growth and removal of poverty are inextricably linked. It is in relation to the development goals in terms of 'quality of life' to the improvement in the living conditions of the poor people, that the potential role and contribution of the construction industry in human settlement programmes and national economic and social development should be seen and appreciated. The concept of social development means that the development process must ensure for all people, access to minimum set of infrastructure facilities and social services, comprising of: (i) shelter, (ii) water supply, (iii) electricity, (iv) transport (v) health and sanitation, (vi) literacy and continuing education. The development strategy must have as its prime goal, the allocation of adequate resources for the growth of a comprehensive social service sector reaching out to all sections of the population within a reasonable period of time.

Construction and National Economy

In the economy of the world today, there is no industry comparable to the construction industry in which from the unskilled labour to the consulting engineer are not to content with serious social and economic problems as are confronting them. Being the industry of 'human well-being' the problems of construction sector are of very real concern to the industry as a whole. It is the construction industry which provides houses, water works, irrigation and sewerage schemes, schools, hospitals, highways, power stations, harbours, airports, factories and cultural amenities and facilities which are so essential for the well-being of the population distributed over hundreds of human settlements, both rural and urban.

The construction sectors serves directly and indirectly, the needs of household in an economy. The direct service is in terms of providing housing, the related facilities and industry as means of production and services through all the other supplying sectors.

Available data indicate that construction is one of the largest sectors of economic activity, second largest to agriculture in the less developed countries and to manufacturing, in more developed countries. The importance of the construction industry in the national economy is determined by its contribution to the Gross Domestic Product (GDP), its direct and indirect impact on other industries and services and its role in capital formation.

Construction and Development

The construction industry is of basic importance to national economic and social development. First, it is a sector which provides most of the economic infra-structure for the manufacturing sector in the form of factories and buildings. Second, it is an instrument by which the benefits of economic development and growth are channelised to the community.

As a country develops, there is an increasing need for more industrial and power projects, housing, community and transport facilities and all other components of an expanding environment in developing human settlements. In India, there is a wide disparity between construction needs and construction capacity which is impeding industrial development and the achievement of national economic and social objectives. Considering that the construction industry consumes a large portion of the locally available materials, provides employment opportunities to a large number of unskilled labour and requires relatively modest capital investment in comparison to other industries, the development of the construction industry should be one of the most important objectives in national economic development plans.

A unique feature of construction industry is that it has a prerequisite to make use of the locally produced materials, right from the early stages of development. As a result, long term programmes are not properly conceived and development priorities cannot be defined clearly. Rather construction is considered merely subsidiary service to other industries.

In the past, construction was considered as an unproductive sector for investment, useful for providing transitional employment for the unskilled labour moving from the rural to urban areas from agriculture to manufacturing. The notion of construction as a means of economic development is gaining ground and the contribution of the construction industry has made it a matter of concern to the Government.

The potentiality of construction industry for meeting redistribution, growth and employment objectives of development have not been adequately explored. Studies have shown that construction industry stands out quite prominently in its income and employment generation potential. Also in terms of income out put and labour output ratios which are of greater relevance in resource allocation. An interesting feature is that all the sectors ranked higher than construction, such as, agriculture, minerals, wood products, non-metallic mineral products and services are related to construction sector throgh their output disposal. This means that any increase in construction activity apart from creating higher direct income and employment per unit of output, would create much higher total income and employment because of inter-industry linkages.

Employment

Construction, a labour intensive industry, which plays a significant role in mitigating the problem of unemployment. By its nature, construction is ideally suited to absorb surplus labour, specially the unskilled.

The construction activity is considered as a complement of industrialisation and the consequent urbanisation so much so that construction activity tends to get concentrated in industrial and urban areas. About 19 to 45 per cent of the total working force is engaged in construction activity. This indicates that, as economic growth proceeds, the share of the secondary and tertiary sector in total employment would tend to rise even as the share of the primary sector in total emplayment declines.

Most of the workers are employees or wage earners, their percentage being as high as 75 to 95 per cent. A disproportionately large number of workers on own account is indicative of the unorganised character of the construction activity.

A sizeable amount of labour is employed in subsidiary industries delivering building materials and components to the construction industry. This should be added to the labour who participate in building activities in the non-monetary sector of the economies i.e. self-help housing. Taking such employment into account it is assumed that construction as such may account for as much as 10 to 16 per cent of the total employment.

In India instability of employment and earning remains a predominant feature of construction activity, which distinguishes it with that of other industries. The nature of the construction industry is such that it experiences the impact of fluctuations more frequently than other sectors.

Being dependent on weather conditions and being a complement to other industries, construction employment is seasonal and intermittent. The construction projects lasts for a limited duration, the construction workers have to move from site to site in order to search for employment. This shifting involves some period of unemployment also. This problem, when coupled with the geographical dispersion of construction activity and its work force may lead to labour shortages or labour surpluses. While the problem of cyclic, seasonal and intermittent unemployment is not unique to construction, in no other industries, are all these sources of instability found at the same time and to the same degree.

Informal Sector

The construction industry which includes housing construction may be classified into (i) formal or modern sector, and (ii) informal or traditional sector. The modern sector which plays an important role in the execution of large scale infrastructural projects and urban development schemes, involves capital intensive technologies and is dominated by large scale construction firms including international building contractors who operate through multinational corporations and enterprises. The informal sector comprises of community building efforts that include activities, such as, self-help construction following traditional construction practices.

It is necessary to provide pre-training to the craftmen in building methods. By employing appropriate training methods, an increasing number of traditionally trained craftsmen in the formal sector may gradually learn to carry out more demanding jobs and many of them may infact, move into the modern sector as skilled workers.

Factor Inputs into Construction

The inputs into construction fall into the following categories :

(i) *Materials and components* which account for 50 to 60 per cent of the total cost of construction;

(ii) *Labour* which accounts for about a third of the cost of construction;

(iii) *Plant and equipment* which may be hired or owned, a change in plant costs being generally proportionate output;

(iv) *Management* the importance of which lies not in the direct costs but in the effect it has on the efficiency of construction and hence, of labour costs and even on material and plant costs; and

(v) *Working capital,* the importance of which is very great not on account of its cost but because contractors may be unable to obtain sufficient working capital at any price to finance construction.

Construction Materials

There are many industries producing materials and components required in the production, maintenance and modernisation of buildings and other construction works. Iron and steel, wood and wood products and plastic industries are among the important suppliers of materials required for building and construction, but as much as half of the total output of iron and steel and wood and wood based industries is consumed for purposes other than construction. On the other hand, materials, such as cement, lime, timber and bricks are produced exclusively for use in construction.

Manpower

Construction industry is one of the largest employers of labour, particularly unskilled labour because of the highly labour intensive nature of its activities. In the early stages of industrialisation, the industry played a role of transitional employer for unskilled labour moving from rural areas to urban centres and from agriculture to manufacturing. In most developing countries there is a high turnover of manual labour and a general low level of skills.

The complexity of the construction operations requires a variety of skills, carpenters, masons, concrete workers, architects, engineers etc. While, unskilled labour is readily available, it is difficult to get skilled workers with adequate knowledge, training and experience.

The relative share of traditional operative skills (such as, masons, carpenters, joiners, concrete mixers and plasterers) has changed rapidly and entirely new skills, such as, structural workers construction mechanics and machine operators are being introduced as a result of innovations in building materials and construction technologies. There is acute shortage of skills, particularly of skilled manpower to meet the growing demand of construction activities.

A major innovation in building technology has been the replacement of massive load-bearing construction by framed structures with relatively limit infill and cladding. The main materials used for frames are currently steel and reinforced concrete. The relative share of different skills in the construction labour force is therefore, changing rapidly following technological changes. The employment of masonary skills is decreasing gradually owing to the use of concrete which has spread more rapidly than any other building techniques.

Equipment

Most construction operations carried out on site using some tools or equipments. Hand tools are in use and have been designed to perform relatively simple and repetitive operations. In this sense, they mostly replace unskilled labour. Mechanisation in the sense of using power driven machines has not been much used for sophisticated operations requiring highly skilled workers who are scarce practically.

Financial and Capital Inputs

The construction process requires sufficient capital resources to bridge the period between inception of the project and the time when it begins to yield its economic or social benefit. This bridge finance is provided by the client whether the client is the government or the private developer, as the case may be. When the government is the client, there is no interest payment made on the capital invested during the bridge period because of the budgetary practices operating in the public sector. But the private developer would have to pay interest on his investment during the bridge period which adds (about 5 to 10 pe rcent) to the capital cost of the building project. This underscores the necessity to cut down the time spent on the construction process. The problem has become increasingly acute with the growing complexity of large scale building projects. The financial facilities available to the construction agencies vary according to the type of the construction agencies. The public limited joint stock construction companies, for example, are able to secure finances in the form of (i) bank advances against immovable and movable assets; (ii) advance payments from clients against machinery and plant brought to site, the amount of advance being limited from 5 to 10 per cent of the contract value; (iii) advances against non-perishable material brought to site to the extent of 50 to 75 per cent of the value of the material, and (iv) private deposits on high rates of interest for short periods.

Management

Construction is essentially an assembly operation involving various inputs of materials, labour, equipment etc., the effective coordination of which is complex and difficult, particularly in large projects. One of the most difficult problems lies in management and organisation of large labour forces. The main concern of construction engineers is for the structure they build while they often show little concern for the construction plant and equipment used in building operations. It cannot be denied that the equipment is an integral part of the construction process and the objective of equipment management should be to achieve maximum unit production at the lowest possible cost. With the induction of heavy equipment into the construction projects, the scheduling and planning of equipment as a resource, has to receive careful attention. Optimum utilisation of equipment, thus, brings in the management aspects of capital investment, depreciation, operation cost, wear and tear, spares inventory, systematic plant maintenance, decisions to make or buy or hire equipment, training of personnel, queing and simulation models for machinery interference etc. The need, therefore, arises for adopting and developing management methods appropriate to local conditions to measure the effectiveness of plant management in terms of lower construction costs and not merely in terms of lower plant costs.

Structure of the Industry

The construction is characterised by the existence of two sectors : a non-monetary traditional sector of the economy consisting of a large number of very small units of an artisan character which operate in the rural and semi-urban areas; and a modern sector consisting of a small number of large firms using modern techniques and organisation, undertaking a major share of the work in urban centres and all of the large infrastructural projects. The modern sector has similar features as in more developed economies with individual building firms generally specialising in a particular type of construction.

Construction is a complex process not only for technological reasons but because large number of participants involved in the complications arising out of their associated interdependence, contractual or otherwise. There are a number of participants involved in construction process; users, clients, designers, manufacturers of building materials, contractors, sub-contractors, building materials dealers etc. Besides, there are also other participants: statutory authorities that must approve the structure, banking financial institutions that advance capital required during and after the construction and public utility undertakings that supply basic services such as electricity, water sewerage etc.

A building industry of the sort described above scarcely exists in many developing countries and is merely the sum of professionals, small contractors and manufacturers which hire workers on an adhoc basis for each project. The gradual development of the building industry among others, is manifested by the size and stability of the construction firms.

Planning and Designing the Construction Activity

Building activities are highly fragmented and at the same time specialised. The industry is highly dispersed geographically and its manpower, equipment and materials are widely used by other industries. One of the major difficulties is the lack of accurate and detailed information and data on many different aspects of the industry. These features make planning difficult and complex task.

The contribution of design to the development of the construction sector is most significant. It is at the design stage that decisions are made as to how materials should be shaped and placed on the building site in order to satisfy the functional requirements. The buildings are designed by construction firms or by the construction independent organisation also.

One of the first tasks of the client is to brief the design team i.e. to define clearly what he expects from the final output. Designing may be done either by professional advisors appointed for the purpose or by a design team employed on contract. The design team may include, depending on the circumstances, architects, engineers, specialists etc. However, such teams are employed on a small proportion of construction work.

The principal functions of the design team is to prepare a set of instructions for the contractor.

Contractors

The bulk of the total construction output is carried out by contractors. In most building work and sometimes even in civil engineering, the main contractor handles only the bulkiest operations connected with the infra-structure (excavation, earth moving foundation etc.) and the superstructure of the building and delegates the more specialised activities connected with finishing and installations to separate firms acting as sub-contractors. The main contractor sub-contracts upto 50 per cent of the total work.

The advantages and need for sub-contracting arrangements in the industry are widely recognised. First, where the sub-contracting involves skilled workers, it is the means by which the industry can obtain the advantages of specialization. These sub-contractors accumulate technical knowledge, specialised equipment and experienced personnel which can make them more efficient in the performance of certain task. Second, for the main contractor, sub-contracting can represent a convenient way of obtaining the services of workers with certain skills. Third, specialised sub-contracting can, to some extent, reconcile the discontinuous need for certain skills on a given construction site with the desire by workers for continuous employment. Specially, sub-contractors constantly search for work that will keep their men and machines fully occupied. Fourth, sub-contracting has also been associated with other forms of productivity advantages such as close supervision, the retention of experienced work teams and the incentive given by contracts which set a fixed lumpsum price for the work to be done. Finally, the work is carried out by labourers from rural areas and where normal channels of recruitment are ill-developed, obtaining a work force through the sub-contractor can offer considerable advantages.

In India, the construction activity is spread throughout the country from the smallest village to the metropolitan city. The smallest unit consists of a headman, leading a team of 5 to 20 workers either skilled or unskilled. The big units are well established corporate bodies employing several engineers, skilled and unskilled workers and also owning heavy and sophisticated construction equipment.

Policies Towards Labour

Employment in the construction industry is discontinuous and subject to constant change in working sites for the labour employed in the construction. A building project has different works and processes all of which do not take place at the same time or continue together for long intervals. Every item of work such as excavation, masonary, concreting, reinforcement work, wood work, finishing etc., are carried out by different workers and their employment restricted only to the duration of that activity.

A significant aspect of the building construction industry is its heavy dependence on migrant labour. The industry employs a large number of casual workers who are outside the purview of protective labour laws which apply to organised labour in other fields. The peculiar nature of employment in the building industry has created enormous problems for building labour, particularly, the unskilled workers including female labour.

The discontinuity of employment has made manpower recruitment and training difficult. It also accounts for generally poor working conditions for labour. In most developing countries, the small size of construction firms, the ease to enter into the industry, the rural background of much of the labour force and the prevalence of too many contracting firms have prevented effective organisation of labour unions.

The responses to the diverse problems created by lack of continuous employment have taken different forms in different countries. Measures have been taken to improve manpower adjustments by expanding permanent employment. Greater employment stability is sought to be achieved through a reduction in the number of firms operating in various parts of the industry. Government manpower services have helped to reduce adjustment problems by orienting training to suit the needs of the industry.

The temporary nature of employment in the construction industry has made it difficult to offer conditions of work similar to those found in other industries. In most developing countries, legislation provides for standards with regard to shelter, dining arrangement, supply of drinking water, toilet facilities, place for cooking, washing and storing, transportion as well as special needs of women workers. In India, the Contract Labour Act regulates the conditions of work and provides for welfare facilities for contract labour in all industries. In actual practices, the requirements of the Act and the safety regulations laid down are rarely met by the contracts. A major shortcoming of the Contract Labour Law is that the implications of the migrant character of building labour has not been adequately appreciated while making general provision for essential facilities and amenities to building labour.

The problems posed by the seasonal and casual nature of employment in building construction require specific attention at the policy and programme levels in terms of undertaking measures for (i) lengthening the period of constructive employment so as to reduce the spells of unemployment to the minimum and (ii) fully or partially decasualising labours so as to ensure stable and continuous employment of labour in the building industry.

Given the unique characteristics of the building industry and the special nature of construction employment, it should be possible to think in terms of orienting the planning and implementation of construction programmes in a manner so as to ensure continuous (in the sense of consecutive) employment of labour in building projects. For, without efforts at employment stabilisation in the construction industry, mere regulatory and control measures as contemplated by the existing Labour Laws will not be effective in providing welfare facilities and amenities to building labour. Experience of implementing the Contract Labour Act has made this abundantly clear.

The objective employment stabilisation could possibly be achieved if steps are taken to create a climate conducive to (i) better organisation of building programmes; (ii) coordinated planning and implementation of constraction programmes, public as well as private; (iii) undertaking repetitive building projects which constitute the core of social and economic infrastructure in the rural and urban areas; (iv) undertaking mass housing construction and (v) undertaking repairs, renewals and rehabilitation of existing housing stock.

Construction Industry and Employment

According to 1981 census, about 222.5 lakh persons were in the labour force in India. In the building and construction industry there were 5.2 lakh workers. According to the available figures 50 per cent of construction workers actually lived in urban settlements while possibly a substantial number commuted seasonally between their village and the construction project site. The number does not include workers in the unorganised sector and petty trades.

Table 3.6

Labour Force in 1981 (In Lakhs)

Labour Force	*In rural areas*	*In urban areas*	*Total*
Total number of workers in the country	176.4	46.1	222.5
Workers in the construction industry (including Dams, bridges, roads etc.)	1.5	1.6	3.1
Workers in the building industry alone	0.9	1.2	2.1

Source : Census 1981.

The role of construction industry as an employment generator is significant as seen below. It must be mentioned that a large amount of construction work is done in the informal sector on the fringes of the monetary economy. This includes construction involving self-help or paid labour and using a wide variety of techniques and a high percentage of local materials.

As is quite evident from the figures, the capacity of one million rupees to employ skilled and unskilled building

Table 3.7

Employment Potential for Rs. 1 Million Investment in Building Industry

	1961	*1971*	*1975*
1. Direct 1.1 skilled and unskilled labour	250	126	87
1.2 supervisory (technical)	9	6	4
1.3 Supervisory	11	7	5
2. *ndirect employment* in building materials and supporting industries	400	200	140
Total	670	339	236

workers has been steadily decreasing over the years. This holds good for the directly employed labour as well as for labour which is indirectly employed in materials production and supporting industries. Reasons for this are many and include the rate of inflation and consequent wage rise for workers, the sensitivity of labour market to national policies regarding agriculture, fiscal policies and incentives etc. About two thirdof the investment in building field goes towards payment of wages to personnel engaged in the building materials production and direct construction activity, etc., while the remaining one third goes towards taxes, land values, profits, etc. The employment potential of building industry on the basis of jobs it provides for housing construction is equally important. Table 3.8, shows the employment capability in direct and indirect activities related to building industry.

It should be noted that the figures relate only to our present modes of construction. In case, some alternative technologies are developed and adopted for housing construction, the figures would change accordingly. Today, since India is constructing only about 0.7 million dwelling units per

Table 3.8

Employment (in Million) in Building Industry at a Construction Rate of One Million Dwelling Units Per Year

1.	Direct employment	
	1.1 skilled labour	0.3
	1.2 unskilled labour	2.2
	1.3 Supervisory (Technical)	0.1
	1.4 Supervisory (non-tech.)	0.1
2.	Indirect employment (in building materials and supporting industries)	
	2.1 Skilled labour	0.5
	2.2 Unskilled labour	3.6
3.	Total	6.8

year, our building industry in the formal sector is able to provide gainful employment only to approximately 5.2 lakh people in the country. A break-up of this figure shows that about 3.1 lakh are employed directly against 2.1 lakh in building industry in 1981.

4

Theoretical Orientation

To work is human nature and women are no exception to it. The work also satisfies human needs and the physical benefits of the work and conditions of work generate feelings and attitudes which determine level of satisfaction or fulfilment of these needs. Every individual adopts various means and methods to fulfil his/her needs which are generally considered short term or long term goals of life. The approach to accomplish these goals determine style of life. In social situations, inspite of individual differences there are certain fixed norms of style of life and under these norms, an individual is expected to work for his livelihood after a certain period of childhood.

In case of women the importance of lower order needs are predominant as they have to, not only look after themselves but nurture the whole family. Many researches have proved that for women the fulfilment of higher order needs is quite satisfactory during pre-marriage period but in the post marriage period the need order is dominated by lower order needs.

Work is a potent source of need fulfilment of various types such as basic needs, security needs, belonging needs, esteem needs and self-actualization. Work is social reality and social expectation to which every person seems to conform, it is a combination of social and biological need gratifier which provides basic amenities for survival and social status which binds every individual to society.

Since the work has related concepts such as working conditions, binding of time, formation of attitude towards unionism etc., these have to be faced as either a support or obstacle in the process of satisfaction of needs derived by individual on the job. Most psychological theorists both, early and contemporary have their roots, at least to some extent, in the principles of need satisfaction and motivation.

A brief description of these theories is presented as follows :

Maslow's Need Hierarchy Theory

Maslow (1954) had suggested that needs are organised hierarchically and that the more basic (lower order) needs in the hierarchy are prepotent, i.e., if a lower level need is not satisfied, its satisfaction is sought before satisfaction of any of the higher level needs.

Maslow's theory in the beginning decade remained primarily in the realm of the clinical psychology but as the attention grew, the need hierarchy theory emerged as theory of work motivation and as an appealing model of human behaviour. A stripped-down version of Maslow's hierarchy of needs was put forward by Alderfer (1969, 1972), combining Maslow's lower two levels into one (existing needs), retaining his middle level (relatedness needs) and combining his top two levels (growth needs), which is widely known as ERG model. McGregor (1960, 1967) popularised this theory and it was widely discussed by organisational theorists and practicing managers.

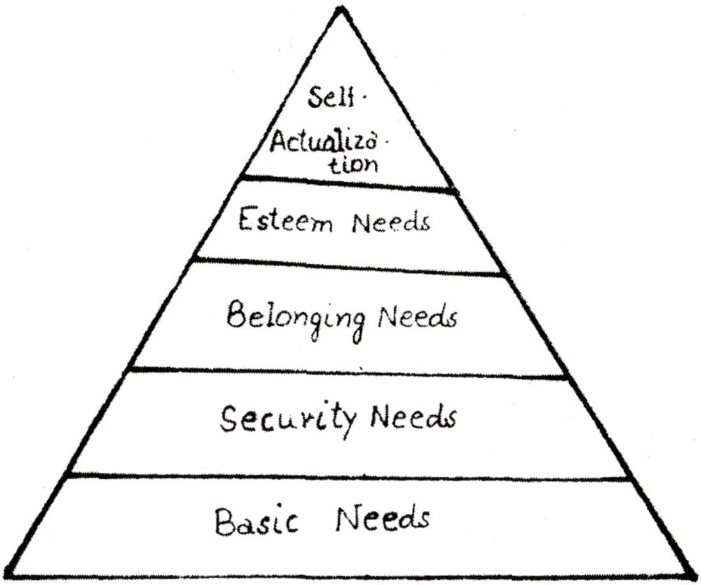

Fig. 4.1 Maslow's Need Hierarchy

In the work settings motivational problems of employees is of a great concern in an organisation. To utilise the full potential of employees, it is necessary to create proper climate. This proper climate may include, the increase in opportunities for greater autonomy, variety, responsibility and so forth. Failure to provide such a climate would hypothetically increase employee frustration and could result in poor performance. Maslow's need hierarchy was tested by Porter's (1964) study on 2000 members of the American Management Association. He administered a 13 item questionnaire based on a modified version of Maslow's hierarchy, aimed at ascertaining the importance of each need, how much it was met and how much it should be met. The study showed that higher level managers place more importance than lower level managers on self-actualisation and autonomy needs.

As shown in the figure above Maslow (1954) posited that most individuals pursue with varying intensities the following needs : (1) basic; (2) security; (3) belonging; (4) esteem and (5) self-actualization.

Those needs which are largely unsatisfied tend to produce tensions within individuals which lead them to behave in a certain fashion in the hope of reducing the tension and restoring internal equilibrium. Once a need becomes satisfied it loses its potency as a motivating force until it again becomes manifest. For example, when a person's physiological needs (say, for food) have been met, they will no longer motivate behaviour until the person again becomes hungry until such time, according to Maslow, the individual would be motivated by other needs. In other words, many of these neede are cyclic.

Unique with Maslow, however, is his second fundamental premise, Specially Maslow argues that the needs which individuals pursue are universal across most populations and that they are arranged sequentially in hierarchical form. That is, once the lower needs are satisfied, the individual moves up in the hierarchy one level at a time and attempts to satisfy the next higher-order needs. The 'physiological needs' are shown first in the hierarchy because they tend to have the highest strength until they are somewhat satisfied. These are basic human needs to sustain life itself—food, clothing, shelter etc. In the context of an organization, these needs are for salary, fringe-benefits and physical working conditions. Until these basic needs are satisfied to the degree needed for the sufficient operation of the body, the majority of person's activity will probably be at this level, and other levels will provide him with little motivation.

One physiological needs are gratified the security needs become predominant. These needs are essentially the need to be free of the fear of physical danger and deprivation of the basic physiological needs. In other words, this is a need for self preservation. In the context of an organization, these needs refer to security in job, management policies and practices etc.

When physiological and security needs are satisfied, social or affiliation needs emerge as dominant in the need structure. Since man is a social being, he has a need to belong and to be accepted by various groups. In the context of an organisation, considerate and supportive supervision, likeable co-workers, etc. When social needs become dominant, a person will strive for meaningful relations with others.

After an individual begins to satisfy his need to belong, he generally wants to be more than just a member of his group. He then feels the need for ego or esteem—both self-esteem and recognition from others. Most people have a need for a high evaluation of themseleves that is firmly based in reality-recognition and respect from others. In an organization context these needs refer to recognition, responsibility, respect etc. on the job. Satisfaction of these esteem needs produce feelings of self-confidence, prestige, power and control.

Once ego or esteem needs begin to be adequately satisfied, the self-actualization needs become more prepotent. This is the need to maximize one's potential, whatever it may be. As Maslow explained it, "what a man can be, he must be." Thus, self-actualization is the desire to become what one is capable of becoming. In an organizational context, these needs are for advancement, interesting work, achievement, etc.

Although the original work of Maslow was in the direction of integration motivation and personality but his theory could be seen in the realm of improving the work environment i.e. improving the quality of working life (QWL) in the work settings. The satisfaction of needs as pointed out by Maslow have a prominent role in the life style of all workers of all cadres. The lowest level of workers are expected to be governed by the lower order needs and various measures may be adopted to improve their QWL to be able to fulfil higher order needs.

Herzberg's Motivation—Hygiene Theory

Whether or not a general factor of job satisfaction exists, has been debated since Herzberg's formulation of a theory of job satisfaction. His theory stems from an analysis of the experiences and feelings of 200 engineers and accountants in nine companies (Herzberg, Mausner and Snyderman, 1959). They were asked to describe job experiences in which they felt exceptionally good or exceptionally bad about their jobs and to rate how much their feelings had been influenced by each experience.

Herzberg et. al. found that favourable job attitudes are usually associated with activities such as achievement, recognition, the work itself, responsibilities and advancement. Unfavourable job attitudes were usually linked with contextual factors such as company policy and administration, supervision and working conditions. The former activities are related to job content, being intrinsic to the job and because of their relation to favourable attitudes, Herzberg called them 'motivators'. He called the environmental factors 'hygiene factors'. He further hypothesised that only motivators could lead to job satisfaction and only hygiene factors to dissatisfaction, i.e. there are two separate dimensions of job satisfaction and job dissatisfaction. Hygiene factors are considered to satisfy the need to avoid pain (i.e. Maslow's lower order need), whereas, motivators are necessary for the satisfaction of self-realisation motives (i.e. Maslow's higher level needs).

The theory has resulted in a number of investigations, some of which support it (e.g. Whitsett and Winslow, 1967), while other's do not (e.g. House and Wigdor, 1967; Dunnette, Campbell and Hake, 1967). The reasons for this lack of support are likely to involve a combination of the following :

(i) supportive studies may be method-bound (i.e. the critical incident technique used by Herzberg may give biased results through a tendency to people to see good experiences as being caused by their own actions and bad experiences as being due to situational (hygiene factors) in so far as people have a need to maintain a positive self-image, then one could expect this to happen;

(ii) even Herzberg's study showed that motivators could be involved in dissatisfaction and hygiene factors in satisfaction, other studies have found this to a great extent (Dunnette et. al., 1967);

(iii) there is some evidence (e.g. Goldthorpe et. al., 1968) that hygiene factors may be important sources of satisfaction as well as dissatisfaction for particular groups of workers, notably 'blue collar' workers; and

(iv) a number of studies suggest that other factors play an important role in determining job satisfaction in particular, the attitude systems and beliefs of the workers concerned.

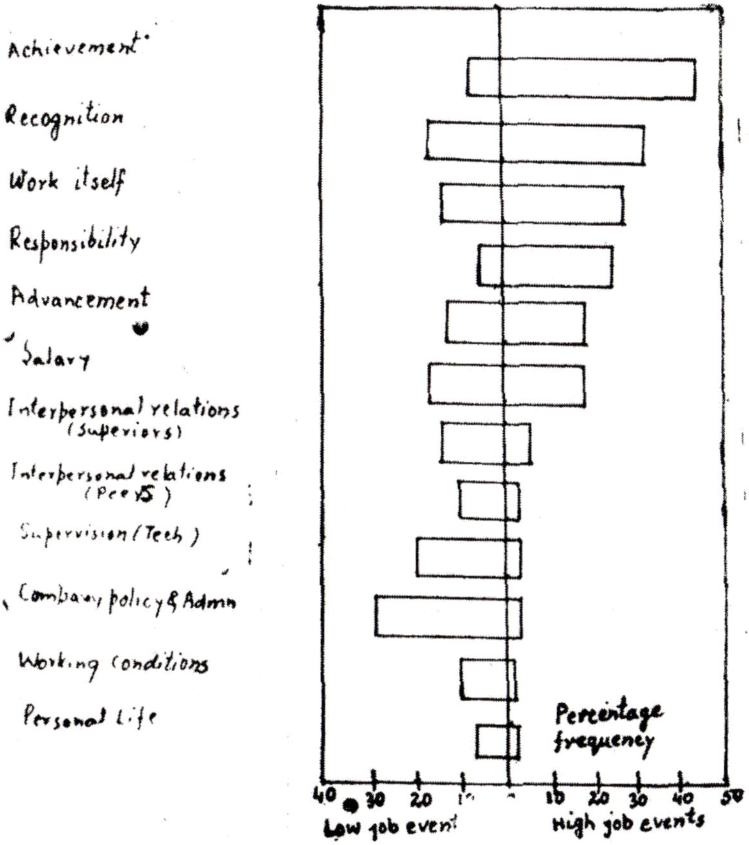

Fig. 4.2 Percentage of High and Low Job Attitude Sequences

Equity Theory

We now come to consideration of relatively recent theory of work motivation called 'equity theory'. While each of the previous theories represent a single line of individual's development indeed is often associated with one individual. The development of equity theory can be traced to several prominent theorists working somewhat independently within the same general parametres. These variations on the theme are variously termed "cognitive dissonance" theory (Festinger, 1957; Heider, 1958) "distributive justice" or "exchange" theory (Homans, 1961; Jacques, 1961; Patchen, 1961), and "equity or inequity" theory (Adams, 1963, 1965; Weick, 1964). While eaeh of these theories differ in some respect from the others, the general thrust of all of them is toward one basic unit of analysis. Specifically, such theories argue that a major determinant of job performance and satisfaction is the degree of "equity" or "inequity", that an individual perceives in a work situation. The degree of equity is defined in terms of a ratio of an individuals inputs (such as effort) to outcomes (such as pay) as compared to similar ratio for a relevant "other". Because of this comparative aspect, the theory has also been called "social comparison theory".

Equity theory concentrates on an understanding of the processes by which behaviour is energized and sustained. It is thus a more dynamic approach to the study of motivationally relevant variables in a work situation. Because of this, equity theory has been called a "process" theory by Campbell et. al. (1970), while the theories of Maslow, Murray and Herzberg have been termed "content" theories.

Equity theory posits that a major share of motivated behaviour is based on the perceived situation and not necessarily on the actual set of circumstances. Where Maslow (1954) and Murray (1938) saw behaviour largely as a result of personality-need variables, Herzberg (1959) saw behaviour as the result of objective job content and job context factors. Equity theory generally argues that it is the perceived equity of the situation that stimulates behaviour and satisfaction. In other words, if an employee "thinks" he is being paid less than his co-workers for the same amount and quality of work, he would according to this theory, be satisfied and would move to reduce the inequity through various means. Such a hypothesis is particularly interesting in view of several findings which indicate that workers generally tend to over estimate the salaries of others (Lowler, 1971).

Theoretical View Point of the Investigation

The theory of need hierarchy pronounced by Maslow seems to be the most suitable to put forth explanation of a number of behaviours of the women construction workers in the work situations in the construction industry. In fact, there are no research evidences available, giving coverage of the behavioural aspects of the work being performed by women in the construction industry. This work, therefore, will be unique in itself which is based on certain presumptions on theoretical grounds provided by Maslow's theory of need hierarchy.

All workers look forward to satisfaction of their needs. The women workers opted for construction work in order to satisfy their basic need to earn money for their survival. The out put of these workers would also depend on satisfaction of this basic need. The insecurity of work and living conditions also play a dominant role in productivity aspect of the workers. The workers also like to earn social prestige, affection from co-workers, supervisors and neighbourers. This need fulfilment is extended to their place of domicile where they like to be recognized as workers of the urban cities.

The workers have a desire to increase their efficiency and reach standards of excellence through the process of skill development. It has been observed that in scarcity of training institutions, the training to the new entrants is provided by a trained and experienced skilled worker in the construction industry. The entrant first serves as unskilled worker, learns basic techniques and then is exposed to lower level skilled work.

The higher level skilled work are gradually exposed. This situation is not true in case of women workers. They enter as unskilled workers and go out as unskilled workers. The present investigation will examine the possibilities of development of skills among women workers.

The development of skills leads to enhancement of earning which helps in satisfaction of higher order needs next to the basic needs. Therefore, if we look at the implication part of the theory, we may find that satisfaction of lower order needs will result in development of higher order needs and their satisfaction will result in higher excellence, productivity and improvement of quality of working life.

The Maslow's theory of need hierarchy may, therefore, serve as a model for improvement of quality of working life for the women workers in the construction industry

5

Methodology

The methodology of any study has to be kept in congruence with the nature of the problem being investigated, its objectives and the category of respondents being interviewed. This part of the study deals with sample, procedures, measuring instruments and statistical analysis of the data.

Sample

The total sample consisted of 220 respondents. All of these respondents were females selected from 22 construction sites located in 5 zones of the Union Territory of Delhi. 4 sites were located in East, 4 in West, 3 in North, 5 in South and 6 construction sites were located in Central Delhi. The selection largely depended upon the intensity of construction activity undertaken in these zones at the time of investigation. In selection of these sites, efforts were made to cover a variety of constructon agencies both public and private which included Central Public Works Department (C.P.W.D.), National Building Construction Corporation, private builders and promoters, individual undertaking construction work independently, etc.

The basic reason for selecting women workers in the unorganized construction sector for the study was in view of their background, social, economic and psychological deprivations leading to a poor quality status. The State laws are also implemented with no effective and controlled measures to supply them the basic amenities and facilities. The social structure keeps them away from any new learning opportunities, either education or occupational training. Certain socio-economic surveys to assess the overall status of women in this sector have been made by the Government as a partof women's decade (1975-85) but have no contents of women's perception of life in the context of their work.

All the studies and the conditions in which these women work elevate them to an oppressed state affecting their quality of working life and number of developmental opportunities.

The performance level of these workers was assessed by 22 immediate supervisors.

There was paucity of information available with regard to total number of construction sites and the number of workers available, on an average on one site, hence, the selection of site was largely, on the basis of quota sampling and from each construction site 10 respondents were selected randomly as per the attendance records of the building contractors/Jamadars.

The sample distribution of various zones in Delhi was as follow:

Zones	*No. of Sites*	*Sample Size*
East	4	40
West	4	40
North	3	30
South	5	50
Central	6	60
Total	22	220

Variables Studied

For the study decision about the independent variables was first scanned through the available research evidences and since, most of the studies have been conducted on higher level workers in a variety of organised sectors, it was felt that the expert opinion invitation was necessary. For this purpose, a panel of experts was contacted and the independent variables were decided.

Similarly, for the dependent variables, the experts were consulted to decide the components of quality of working life. The following paradigm depicts the independent and dependent variables:

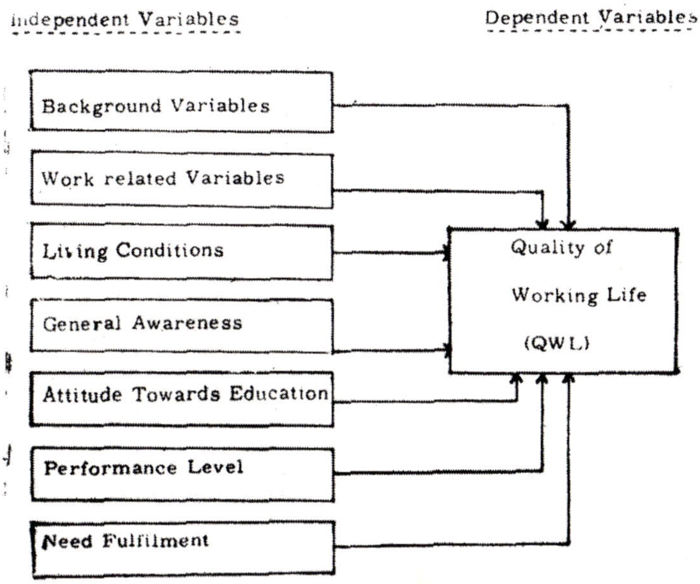

Background Variables

The background variables include age, caste, religion, marital status, migration category, state of migration, education status, family size, family type, personal income, husband's income, per-capita income etc.

Work-related Variables

The work-related variables included satisfaction from own work, husband's occupation, income, occupational category, work experience, number of family members in construction work, liking of skilled works, preference of skilled works (within and out of construction activity), motivation to learn skills, role conflicts, condition of equipments, need for improvement, cooperation from co-workers and supervisor.

Living Condition Variables

The variables regarding living conditions of the women construction workers were largely confined to basic services, such as living space, availability of water supply, electricity, payments, public conveniences, medical and health services ration card, security arrangements, child care centres etc.

General Awareness

The general awareness of the women construction workers included knowledge about surroundings and some of the concerned laws about equal wages etc. Both aided and unaided awareness were considered as general awareness.

Attitude Towards Education

The attitude of the women workers towards education was measured by constructing an attitude scale which had nine items. Each item was evaluated by the respondents on a three point scale. The total score obtained was considered as attitude towards education.

Performance Level

The performance level was assessed by the immediate supervisors of the women workers on 14 of its components which were physical strength, daily out-put, perfection in work, quality of work, obedience, regularity of work, understanding the job, coordination of work, relation with co-workers, relation with supervisor, overcoming problems independently, learning of new works, interest in work and overall performance. These dimensions were assessed on a five point scale and the total score was also calculated.

Need Fulfilment

The need hierarchy of Maslow (1954) was also evaluated in terms of the five needs i.e. basic needs, security needs, belonging needs, esteem needs and self-actualisation, for which the women workers generally look forward in the working situation. The need was assessed in terms of what it is now and what it should be?

These independent variables could be classified into two main categories i.e. (i) conditions (ii) feelings, conditions represent the variables which narrate existing situations or conditions and may be considered as objective indicators of quality of working life and the feelings are considered as psychological reactions to various situations and may be categorised as subjective indicators of quality of working life.

Measuring Instruments

Construction of the measuring instruments was a special task because of certain obvious background details of the respondents. The women workers in construction industry are generally illiterates with very low level of comprehension and reasoning. Therefore, the instruments were required to be designed in such a manner that empirical responses are recorded with minimum of strain to the respondents.

Generally, as per the literature available, quality of working life studies have been conducted on workers belonging to higher cadres that too in the organised sectors and the instruments used have been designed suited to the background, comprehension and reasoning abilities of the respondents but attempts to study lowest order of workers in the unorganised sector have been recorded almost negligible.

The respondents were approached in a face to face situation with an interview schedule developed on the basis of informal interviews with women construction workers, their husbands and number of other concerned persons such as sub-contractor, employer etc. The pilot study also helped in the process and structuring of the schedule more systematically. Even for the variables such as attitude towards education, need fulfilment and quality of working life, face to face interview technique was used.

As per the variables of the study, five (A, B, C, D and E) structured interview schedules were prepared in Hindi using colloquial language.

A. Background, Living Condition, Work-related Conditions and General Awareness Schedule

This Schedule contained information regarding personal bio-data of the women workers, various aspects of the living conditions, working conditions—occupational information choices and preferences, dual role conflicts and general awareness items which were largely regarding basic environmental knowledge and basic laws of work.

B. Attitude Towards Education Scale

A three point scale was used against items related to attitude towards education, both positive and negative items were included. These items were selected out of 26 items in the pilot study by Likert's method of attitude scale construction.

C. Need Fulfilment Questionnaire

Every individual in the work setting expects some of his/her needs to be satisfied. For this questionnaire, Maslow's (1954) need hierarchy was used which included five needs i.e. basic, safety, belonging, esteem and actualization needs. For the present study, need fulfilment questionnaire developed by Porter (1961), was adopted and modified in the context of illiterate women workers and their work situations was used for the measurement of need hierarchy. It consisted of 15 items, with 5 point rating scale, ranging from maximum to minimum and this rating was obtained at two levels: How much it is there now? and How much it should be? The maximum score in this could be plus 4 and minimum, minus 4 for each item. In the questionnaire 3 items measured one particular need, hence, for each of the need an average score was calculated on the basis of the two differential scores on each item. The idea of using the adopted modified Need Fulfilment Questionnaire was to facilitate understanding on the part of the illiterate women workers.

Percentage of judge's agreement with regard to each need was found out and items having agreement between 70 to 100 per cent were selected.

Reliability of the Need Fulfilment Questionnarie

The test-retest reliability coefficients of the Need Fulfilment Questionnaire was calculated which are presented in Table 5.1.

The test-retest reliability of the Need Fulfilment Questionnaire was determined by administering the test on the same subjects with a time interval of four weeks. The test-retest reliability has been found to be 0.72 (N=50), with an index of reliability of 0.85.

Table 5.1

Test-retest Reliability Estimation of the Need Fulfilment Questionnaire

N	*Correlation Coefficient of the half test*	*Esteem of reliability coefficients for total test*	*Index of reliability*
50	0.56	0.72	0.85

It can be seen from Table 5.1 that the test-retest reliability of the Need Fulfilment Questionnaire is very high after correction. The obtained value of correlation is significant at 0.001 level. This result compare favourably with the reliability reported in the past studies for the Need Fulfilment Questionnaire. While the test-retest reliability coefficients suggested considerable evidence for reliability of the Need Fulfilment Questionnaire.

Validity of the Need Fulfilment Questionnaire

The face validity of the Need Fulfilment Questionnaire appears to be fairly high as the stens of the items were prepared, following interviews of 50 respondents regarding various aspects of their concept of need fulfilment.

Content validity is adequately assured as only those items have been selected for the final Need Fulfilment Questionnaire for which there was a high degree of agreement (between 70 to 100 per cent) among the 20 judges, who were professional sociologists and psychologists. This has given a high consensual validity of the Need Fulfilment.

D. Schedule for Measuring Performance Level

In this schedule the performance ratings on 14 items as mentioned earlier was obtained from the immediate supervisors which ranged from very good to very poor. A total score was also calculated.

E. Quality of Working Life Inventory

The QWL inventory had 18 items related to the job conditions which included items on independent actions, control on work, interpersonal relations, developmental opportunities and comprehension of work. The items also included psychological feelings of women workers towards their own position in respect of their own occupation in the construction industry.

Of course, the development of the QWL inventory was based on individual indepth interviews and observations of the researcher and other experts in the field, but it may be compared with the questionnaire developed by Sashkin and Lengermann later in 1984. Their questionnaire on QWL has a complex procedure of scoring each of the component of QWL and is suitable for higher level workers/executives only.

The scoring procedure for the questionnaire developed to measure perception of QWL by women construction workers had well structured items on a three point scale : 'satisfled', 'not sure', and 'not satisfied'. A combined score was derived out of all 18 responses.

Reliability of the QWL

The split-half and test-retest reliability coefficients of the QWL was calculated, as can be seen from Table 5.2.

The scores on first nine and the last nine items for the entire QWL inventory was correlated using the product moment method. The split-half-reliability, applying Spearman-Brown formula for doubling the test has been found to be 3.76 with an index of reliability of 0.87, as evident from Table 5.2.

Table 5.2

Split-half and Test-retest Reliability Estimation of the QWL

B	*N*	*Correlation coefficients for the half test/first administration of the test*	*Estimate of Reliability coefficients for the total test*	*Index of reliability*
Split-half reliability	50	0.62	0.76	0.87
Test-retest reliability		0.67	0.80	0.89

As can be seen in Table 5.2 the split-half reliability of first and second half scores of QWL based on split-half of the 18 items was found very high after correction. The two correlations were significant at 0.0001 level. The split-half reliability of the QWL is encouraging enough to suggest the use of the total scores on QWL as a reliable index, amenable for all meaningful statistical analysis and interpretation.

The test-retest reliability of the QWL was determined by administering the test to the same set of respondents with a time gap of three weeks. The test-retest reliability has been found to be 0.80 (N = 50) with an index of reliability of 0.89.

The test-retest reliability of the QWL is very high after correction. The correlations are significant at 0.001 level. These results compared favourable with the reliability reported in the past studies of the quality of work life instrument. While both split-half and test-retest reliability coefficients suggest considerable evidence for reliability of the QWL.

Validity of the QWL

The face validity of the QWL inventory appeared to be fairly high as the stens of the items were prepared following interviews of 100 subjects regarding the various aspects of their concept of quality of working life. It had to be done in two stages. In the first stage, the researcher did rating himself and at the second stage inter-rater agreement on each ofthe item of the QWL instrument was obtained from 20 judges who were professional in the field of sociology and psychology.

Content validity is adequately assured as only those items have been selected for the final QWL, for which there was a high degree of agreement (between 70 to 100 per cent) among the 20 judges. This has given a high consensual validity to the QWL instrument.

Procedure

Before using the instrument a pilot study was conducted on 40 women workers and their ratings of performance level were obtained from four of their immediate supervisors.

For the purpose of the final study, 220 women construction workers were selected from 5 zones of Delhi. The present study was restricted to Delhi only because the workers migrate from the drought-prone rural areas in search of work to the urban centres for the search of employment and this basic feature is common for all urban centres. The immediate employment available to them is in the construction industry through a sub-contractor or a middle man.

Attempts were made to contact Revenue Department of Delhi Administration, Delhi Development Authority, Central Public Works Department to obtain a comprehensive list of all the construction sites, at the time of investigation but because of lack of inter-organizational coordination, the list could not be made exhaustive. However, the selection of the sites was left to the choice of the researcher so that all categories of construction sites could be covered for the study. As per the sample size shown earlier, 22 sites were selected from 5 zones of Delhi and from each site 10 women workers were selected randomly as per the attendace records available with the contractor.

Face to face interviews were conducted after working hours i.e. in evenings, in three to four sittings. Since the time available with women workers is limited during the working hours and the employer would never be ready to allow the workers to be involved with any other activity, approach was made at home. At residential sites also the group of these workers is looked after by the labour contractor whom they call 'Jamadar'. At first instance, approach was made to the Jamadar to introduce the researcher to the workers but it was not quite successful. The site engineers or project managers were approached and then they granted the permission to the concerned Jamadar to enable conduct of the indepth interviews. investigator.

At many occasions the permission was refused because the workers were involved with overtime work or an important phase of work.

While talking to the workers, care was taken to create homely atmosphere and the worker was not distructed from her daily routine work. Some interviews were conducted while the women workers were either cooking their food or taking care of their children.

Statistical Analysis of Data

After the data were collectcd, each of the interview schedule was screened and for each of the instrument used, appropriate methods were used to score them.

Scoring Procedure for QWL Inventory

As stated earlier a common score was derived out of the 18 items related to various job conditions and pschological feelings towards self and own occupation. All 18 items were rated on a three point scale. The positive items were scored from positive to negative side and the negative items were scored from negative to positive side.

Scoring Procedure for Attitude Towards Education Scale

Nine items were selected to measure attitude towards education of the women workers on a three point scale. A common score was derived out of all the nine responses.

Scoring Procedure for Performance Level Assessment Schedule

The assessment was made by the supervisors on a five point scale. There were 14 dimensions which were independent of each other and related to the working aspects on the construction site. A total score was calculated on the basis of the total of all the scores obtained on each dimension. The maximum score could be 70 and minimum 14.

Scoring Procedure for General Awareness Questionnaire

The general awareness questionnaires contained 10 items of general nature regarding nearest environment, basic facilities, etc. In case, the respondent was aware she was awarded two scores for it and if not aware one. The maximum score, therefore, could be 20 and the minimum 10.

The background information, living condition information and the informations regarding work related conditions were largely objective in nature. Wherever applicable rating scale was used.

Statistical Analysis

After the data were collected from the field, it was subjected to coding into appropriate columns for the purpose of computerisation,

Apart from the univariate, bivariate and multivariate analysis of data, and percentage analysis were used. The percentage analysis has been reported for all the inquiries made in the detailed interview schedule as the first step. The analysis was done for the total sample to explore the relationship of QWL with background factors, attitude towards education, work related factors, living conditions, general awareness, performance appraisal and need fulfilment.

Product Moment Correlations for all the variables in all sub-groups as well as for the total sample were computed for univariate and bivariate statistical analysis.

The students 't' ratios were computed to decide, if the difference existed between the means of two groups. This distribution can be used to determine the probability of obtaining a difference of a given magnitude between two means as result of sampling error. The student 't' distribution helped in reaching at a rational decision.

The Chi-square test, a non-parametric test of association was also computed. The chi-square test involves both a probability interpretation and a measure of reliability of comparing observed frequency distributions with expected distributions. Introduced by Pearson (1900), the Chi-square test probably is the best known and the most important of all non-parametric methods. Because the test makes no assumption about the population being sampled. The Chi-square test can be used to test any hypothesis regarding the expected frequency of events.

From among multivariate techniques, multiple regression was used to find out effects of selected independent variables on the dependent variables. In this study, a stepwise regression analysis has been used with QWL as criterion variable to get the composite weightage of some of the other variables on QWL for total sample.

In stepwise regression, a likely single independent variable is related to the dependent variable through a regression equation. If their partial coefficients show that they make a singificant contribution, variables are tested. A stepwise procedure thus allows the data to tell their own story in terms of empirical first order interrelationship. Multiple correlations also have been computed for predictor variables in stepwise order. B, Beta Weight, Standard Error of B and 'F' ratios were also calculated.

With the above methodological approach, various statistical techniques and research instruments used, the data was collected from respondents and analysed to explore the relationship of QWL with the aforesaid variables.

6

Results and Interpretations

As mentioned in Chapter 5, various techniques of data analysis were used and the proposed hypothesis were tested. This Chapter consists of findings of the study and their relevant discussion in the light of previous researches. It may be pointed out at this stage only that exact relevant researches, in which workers of the category of women workers in construction industry studied on QWL as criterion variable, were not found as reported in the Chapters on literature review, wherever possible, the findings have been compared with the existing researches.

The findings have been presented in the following order :

1. Analysis of Selected Background Variable and their Relationship with QWL.
2. Analysis of Selected Work-related Variables and their Relationship with QWL.
3. Relationship of selected Living Condition Variables with QWL.
4. Relationship of General Awareness with QWL.

5. Relationship of Attitude Towards Education with QWL.
6. Analysis of Performance Level and their Relationship with QWL.
7. Relationship of Need Fulfilment with QWL.

1. Analysis of Selected Background Variables and their Relationship with QWL

In order to study relationship between some selected background variables, Pearson's product moment correlations were computed which have been presented in Table 6.1.1.

Non Paramatic Chi-square test (Siegal, 1956) of significance was also conducted for variables which had probable association with QWL, on the basis of the frequency of respondents in high and low QWL groups. The median value of 35 determined these groups.

Multiple regression analysis was also run to identify predictor background variables of QWL.

Hypothesis I

The hypothesis states that there will be no relationship of background variables with QWL. Since it is a null hypothesis all variables under background variables were seen in the same context.

(*a*) *Age*

To test relationship of age of the women workers with QWL, product moment correlation was computed. The value of correlation coefficient was found to be 0.044 which was not significant at 0.05 level (Table 6.1.2). The coefficient, therefore, indicated that no significant relationship existed between age of the respondents and QWL.

The Chi-square test of significance (Table 6.1.3) also showed that there was no association of age with high and low QWL group of respondents.

Table 6.1.1

Intercorrelations Among Selected Background Variables

Sr. No.	Background Variables	1	2	3	4	5	6	7	8	9	10	11	12	13	14
1.	Age	1	09	—04	—02	—02	—07	08	45*	—29**	33**	08	—01	02	—16*
2.	Caste		1	05	18*	—12	—04	16*	18*	05	04	05	—05	—20*	—08
3.	Religion			1	—06	04	00	—14	—02	—06	—13	—06	—02	01	—06
4.	Marital Status				1	—23**	02	27**	09	59**	09	—08	—05	—37**	—19*
5.	Migration Category					1	31**	—06	—07	—11	—04	—15	38**	01	13
6.	Education Status						1	06	—05	06	03	27**	00	16*	17*
7.	Family Type							1	31**	24**	38**	13	01	—30**	01
8.	Family Size								1	—08	03	03	03	—12	—33**
9.	Husband's Occupation									1	—03	14	—02	—10	—06
10.	Average Family Age										1	02	—02	—08	17*
11.	Average Family Education											1	—09	15	07
12.	Personal Monthly Income												1	—04	19*
13.	Husband's Monthly Income													1	44**
14.	Per-capita Monthly Family Income														1

p<.05r=0.161 *Significant at .05 level

p<.01r=0.211 **Significant at .01 level

All decimals have been removed other than the diagonals.

Table 6.1.2

Intercorrelations between Selected background Variables and QWL

Sr. No.	*Background Variables*	*'r' with QWL*
1.	Age	0.044 NS
2.	Caste	0.042 NS
3.	Migration Category	—0.152*
4.	Educational Status	—0.168*
5.	Family Type	0.045 NS
6.	Family Size	0.047 NS
7.	Average Family Age	—0.055 NS
8.	Average Family Education	0.057 NS
9.	Per Capita Monthly Family Income	—0.213**

*Significant at .05 level **Significant at .01 level.

NS = Not Significant

Table 6.1.3

***Bivariate Frequency Distribution of Respondents Classified in terms of their Age and Quality of Working Life**

Variable	*Quality of Working Life*		*Total*
Age	*High (Score 35 and above)*	*Low (Score below 35)*	
Upto 20 years	21(9.5)	16(7.3)	37(16.8)
21-25 years	27(12.3)	37(16 8)	64(29.1)
26-30 years	19(8.6)	31(14.1)	50(22.7)
31-40 years	15(6.8)	30(13.6)	45(20.5)
Above 40 years	10(4.5)	14(6.4)	24(10.9)
Total	92(41.8)	128(58.2)	220(100)

Chi-square : 5.03 Degree of freedom : 4

Significance level : 0.28

*Figures shown in parenthesis refer to marginal percentage.

The variable was further examined by mutilple regression analysis to know if it was the predictive variable of QWL. Table 6.1.4 shows 'F' ratios of background variables, taking QWL as criterion variable.

If we look at age specific participation percentage of women workers (Table 1.1 in Appendix), we may find that about 84 per cent of the respondents were falling in the age range of 16-40 years. The distribution of the respondents is somewhat near equal in both high and low QWL group. It may, therefore, be said that since age was not important in the work situation for women construction workers, rather physical strength to do unskilled, load bearing work was more important.

Supporting the finding Mishra (1985) while working on managerial level workers found that age was not a factor affecting QWL. Mehta (1976) stated that increase in age leads to work related satisfaction among supervisory staff, managers and Government officials. George (1984) found significant relationship between age and QWL among managerial level workers. Ghosh and Kalra (1982) also found that employee welfare was influenced by age.

The sub hypothesis is, therefore, accepted that age has no relationship with QWL.

(*b*) *Caste*

To find out the relationship between caste and the QWL of the respondents, product moment correlation was computed. The value of the coefficient of correlation was 0.042 (Table 6.1.2). This value was not significant at .05 level. This shows that there is no relationship between caste and QWL.

The percentage analysis of caste shows that 51.8 per cent of the respondents were Scheduled Castes, only 8.2 per cent were Scheduled Tribes and 40.0 per cent of respondents belonged to other castes which were Rajputs, Brahmins and Muslims also (Table 1.2 in Appendix). The representation of the Scheduled Tribes is comparatively lower which may be

Table 6.1.4

B, Beta Weight, Standard Error of "B" Multiple R, R Square and 'F' Ratio in Multiple Regression Analysis for Background Variables as Significant Predictors of Quality of Working Life

Sr. No.	*Background Variable*	*B*	*Beta Weight*	*Standard Error of 'B'*	*Multiple R*	*R Square*	*"F" Ratio*
1.	Age	0.32	0.07	0.18	0.04	0.00	3.10 NS
2.	Caste	0.39	0.03	0.33	0.05	0.00	1.37 NS
3.	Migration Category	—0.36	—0.03	0.38	0.15	0.02	0.92 NS
4.	Educational Status	—0.41	—0.04	0.35	0.22	0.05	1.41 NS
5.	Family Type	0.60	0.05	0.51	0.44	0.20	1.37 NS
6.	Family Size	—0.15	—0.03	0.18	0.22	0.05	0.72 NS
7.	Average Family Age	—0.13	—0.02	0.19	0.23	0.05	0.46 NS
8.	Average Family Education	0.38	0.03	0.35	0.05	0.06	0.13 NS
9.	Per Capita Monthly Family Income	—0.14	—0.02	0.24	0.29	0.08	0.34 NS

NS : Not Significant

due to availability of tribal occupations of this population within their place of domicile.

It may, therefore, be said that caste has no significant relation with QWL and accept the sub hypothesis. The multiple regression analysis shows that the value of 'F' ratio in case of caste was found to be 1.37 which was insignificant at .05 level. This showed that caste is not a significant predictor of QWL.

(*c*) *Migration Category*

For finding out relationship of migration category of the women workers with that of QWL, product moment correlation was computed. The value of the coefficient of correlation was found to be —0.152 which was significant at 0.05 level. This is indicative of the fact that migration category of the women construction workers had relationship with QWL. The minus value of the figure indicated that permanent migrants tend to have better perception of QWL.

In the percentage analysis it has been observed that the women workers in the construction industry migrate from drought-prone areas of the rural agricultural fields to a nearby urban centre. Some of them settle permanently in the urban areas (32.3 per cent) but some revert back to their agriculture profession and participate in construction activity for a specific period in a year (Table 1.5 in Appendix).

Migration is a special feature of construction workers, the research evidences do not have any mention of QWL studies on migrant workers. The finding show that permanent migrants may have settled way of life and their living conditions may be stable which provided feeling of satisfaction.

Of course, migratory category of the respondents is related to QWL but it was not found to be a significant predictor of QWL.

Therefore, we may partially accept the sub hypothesis.

(*d*) *Educational Status*

For determining the relationship of educational status of the women workers with QWL, product moment correlation was computed. The value of the coefficient of correlation was found to be —0.168 which was found significant at 0.05 level. The figure, therefore, indicated that educational status of the women workers is related to QWL. The minus value indicated that even less educated workers may have high QWL (Table 6.1.2).

The percentage analysis showed that most of the respondents were illiterates having no exposure to education at any stage of their life (92.7 per cent), however, 5.5 per cent respondents had an exposure of education uptil 3rd standard and about 1.8 per cent studied uptil 5th standard and beyond.

In the multiple regression analysis, the value of 'F' ratio obtained was 1.41 which was found insignificant at 0.05. This showed that educational status was not the predictor variable of QWL.

The studies on illiterate workers with the objective to find out relationship with QWL are absent, however, Mishra (1985) reported that in case of higher level managers, higher the education, higher may be the QWL perception. Mehra (1984) did not find level of education related to need fulfilment and job involvement. Ahmed (1971), Ashraf (1975) found that low level of education of employees leads to dissatisfaction.

In lieu of the above discussion, it may be stated that the sub hypothesis stands true. What seems to be more important was not actual acquiring of education but realizing value of education which may be useful for the future generation of the women workers.

(*e*) *Family Type*

The examination of the relationship between family type with QWL was done by computing product moment correlation. The value obtained was 0.045. This value was not found significant at 0.05 level. This indicated that no relationship existed between the two variables (Table 6.1.2).

The Chi-square test of association was also applied to determine association of family type with high and low QWL groups of respondents as shown in Table 6.1.5.

Table 6.1.5

***Bivariate Frequency Distribution of Respondents Classified in Terms of Family Type and QWL**

Variable	*Quality of Working Life*		*Total*
Family Type	*High (Score 35 and above)*	*Low (Score below 35)*	
Nuclear	67(30.4)	87(39.6)	154(70.0)
Joint	25(11.4)	41(18.6)	66(30.0)
Total	92(41.8)	128(58.2)	220(100.0)

Chi-square : 0.39 Degree of freedom : 1
Significance level : 0.53
**Figure shown in parenthesis refer to marginal percentage*

The multiple regression analysis showed that the value of 'F' ratio was not significant which meant that family type was not found as a significant predictor of QWL.

Nuclear family is a new concept to migrant workers. Some of the workers are quite adjusted and some are yet to develop measures of adjustment. Workers in the construction industry generally migrate from rural areas to urban areas as a whole family and are yet to conceptualize advantages and disadvantages of the family type. This, therefore, may have shown no relationship with QWL. The sub hypothesis is, therefore, accepted.

(*f*) *Family Size*

The product moment correlation computed between family size of the respondents and the QWL was found to be

0.047 which was not significant (Table 6.1.2). This indicated that there is no relationship between family size of the respondents and the QWL.

The Chi-square test also indicated insnigificant association of family size with high and low QWL groups.

Table 6.1.6

***Bivariate Frequency Distribution Respondents Classified in Terms of Family Size and QWL**

Variable	*Quality of Working Life*		*Total*
Family size (No. of Family members)	*High (Score 35 and above)*	*Low (Score below 35)*	
Two only	11(5.0)	16(7.3)	27(11.3)
Three only	25(11.4)	19(8.6)	44(20.0)
Four only	27(12.3)	41(18.6)	68(30.9)
Five only	20(9.1)	27(12.3)	47(21.4)
Six and above	9(4.1)	25(11.4)	34(15.5)
Total	92(41.8)	128(58.2)	220(100.0)

Chi-square : 7.51 Degree of freedom : 4

Significance level : 0.11

*Figures shown in parenthesis refer to marginal percentage

The multiple regression analysis gave the value of 'F' ratio as 0.72 in case of family size which was insignificant. It may, therefore, be said that family size was not found as predictor variable of QWL.

The average family size was found to be four members in a family. In the illiterate masses no realization of family size existed and they do not cosider it as a problem affecting their work life. This may be the reason of no relation between family size and QWL. Hence, the sub-hypothesis was accepted.

(*g*) *Average Family Age*

In order to examine relationship of average family age with QWL, product moment correlation was computed. The value of the corretation coefficient obtained was 0.055 which was found insignificant (Table 6.1.2). This indicated that the two variables were not related to each other.

The value of 'F' ratio was computed which also indicated that the variable was not predicting QWL. The sub-hypothesis is therefore, accepted.

(*h*) *Average Family Education*

The value of the correlation coefficient was computed to examine the relationship of average family education with QWL. The value obtained was 0.057 which was insignificant at 0.05 level. This indicated that there was no relationship between the two variables.

The multiple regression analysis showed that this variable was also not predicting QWL, hence, sub-hypothesis is accepted (Table 6.1.4).

(*i*) *Per-capita Monthly Family Income*

To determine the relationship of per-capita monthly family income of the respondents with QWL, product moment correlation was computed. The value obtained was —0.213 which was found significant at 0.01 level. The result, therefore, indicated that per-capita monthly family income of the respondents was related to QWL. The minus value of the correlation coefficient indicated that even lower per-capita monthly family income may have high QWL (Table 6.1.2).

The value of Chi-square (9.75) indicated that it was significant at 0.05 level. This shows that there was significant association between per-capita monthly family income and QWL.

Table 6.1.7

***Bivariate Frequency Distribution of the Respondents Classified in Terms of Per-Capita Monthly family Income and QWL**

Variable	*Quality of Working Life*		*Total*
Per-capita Monthly Family Income	*High (Score 35 and above)*	*Low (Score below 35)*	
Upto Rs. 100	9(4.1)	26(11.8)	35(15.9)
Rs. 101-200	43(19.5)	64(29.1)	107(48.6)
Rs. 201-300	27(12.3)	32(14.5)	59(26.8)
Above Rs. 300	13(5.9)	6(2.7)	19(8.6)
Total	92(41.8)	128(58.2)	220(100.0)

Chi-square : 9.75 Degree of freedom : 3
Significance level : 0.02
* Figures shown in parenthesis refer to marginal percentage

Of course, the Chi-square value was significant, indicating the relationship of QWL with per-capita monthly family income but it was not found significant predictor of QWL in the multiple regression analysis.

George (1984) found significant relation between income and QWL while Mishra (1985) also observed the same trend in his study on high level workers. Ghosh and Kalra (1982) found income influencing welfare of employees.

The trend of researches and the present findings reject the sub-hypothesis.

2. Analysis of Selected Work-related Variables and their Relationship with QWL.

To examine the relationship of some selected work related variables, mainly three statistical exercises were performed. First, computation of product moment correlation.

Second, application of chi-square test of significance and the third was multiple regression analysis. The variables selected were. tenure of work experience, number of family members involved in construction work, willingness to become skilled workers, cooperation from co-worker, cooperation from supervisor, satisfaction from own work, husband's occupation and income. The inter-correlation among the these variables is shown in Table 6.2.1.

Hypothesis II

The hypothesis states that the relationship of work-related variables will not be significant with QWL.

The selected work related variables have been seen in the light of the hypothesis II and have been tested as independent sub-hypotheses.

(*a*) *Tenure of Work Experience*

To examine the relationship of tenure of work experience with QWL, product moment correlation was computed. The value of the coefficient of correlation was found to be 0.099 which was not significant at 0.05 level. This, therefore, suggested that no relationship existed between the two variables (Table 6.2.2).

The value of Chi-square obtained was 1.45 and it was found insignificant at 0.05 level. This shows that there was no association between tenure of work experience and QWL.

The multiple regression analysis yielded 'F' ratio as 0.02, in case of tenure of work experience. This value was not found significant. It may, therefore, be said that tenure of work experience was not predicting QWL significantly (Table 6.2.4).

Work experience in studies on high level workers have shown positive signs of relationship with QWL (Ghosh and Kalra, 1982) whereas Singh and Magg (1980) found that income and experience do not significantly affect perception of QWL.

Table 6.2.1

Intercorrelations Among Selected Work-Related Variables

Sr. No.	Work-Related Variables	1	2	3	4	5	6	7	8	9	10	11	12	13	14	15	16
1.	Occupation in Construction Work	1	07	10	02	—07	—03	—08	—08	04	—11	—09	—02	—03	07	00	—02
2.	Tenure of Work Experience		1	10	—11	01	—16*	12	05	08	23	09	11	01	11	09	12
3.	Number of Family Members involved in construction			1	—01	15	01	07	—14	06	—10	—15	—7*	14	—15	06	—15
4.	Skilled Work liked				1	—04	24**	—10	—07	—03	—10	—09	—20	—19*	96	09	08
5.	Out of Construction Skills liked					1	07	—02	08	06	05	04	16	—03	—12	—24**	—08
6.	Willingness to Become Skilled Worker						1	—06	03	—11	—08	—02	—10	—17**	04	02	04

7. Reasons for not Becoming Skilled Worker	1	05	12	—03	01	11	—01	—02	08	—03
8. Skilled Work Known		1	11	05	23**	—01	—09	—10	—11	—21**
9. Problems of Dual Role Performing			1	07	08	20	32**	10	—01	—20*
10. Work (Const./ Household Liked				1	22**	14	18**	—08	—02	—06
11. Condition of Equipments					1	12	09	03	05	—01
12. Cooperation from Co-workers						1	40**	17*	04	08
13. Cooperation from Supervisor							1	02	04	—04
14. Satisfaction from Own Work								1	36**	54**
15. Satisfaction from Husband's occupation									1	18*
16. Satisfcation from Income										1

$p \triangleleft .05$ $r = 0.161$ *Significant at .05 level. ** Significant at .01 level.

$p \triangleleft .01$ $r = 0.211$ All decimals have been removed other than diagonals.

Table 6.2.2

Inter Correlations Between Work Related Variables and Quality of Working Life

Sr. No.	*Work Related Variables*	*'r' with QWL*
1.	Tenure of Work experience	0.099 NS
2.	Number of family members involved in construction	–0.030 NS
3.	Willingness to become skilled worker	–0.228**
4.	Cooperation from co-workers	0.230**
5.	Cooperation from supervisor	0.139 NS
6.	Satisfaction from own work	–0.015 NS
7.	Satisfaction from husband's occupation	–0.035 NS
8.	Satisfaction from income	–0.131 NS

** Significant at .01 level.   NS: Not significant

Table 6.2.3

***Bivariate frequency Distribution of Respondents Classification in Terms of their Tenure of work Experience and Quality of working life**

Variables	*Quality of Working Life*		*Total*
Tenure of Work Experience	*High (Score 35 and above)*	*Low (Score below 35)*	
Upto 2 years	41(18.6)	51(23.2)	92(41.8)
3-4 years	23(10.5)	28(12.7)	51(23.2)
5 years and above	28(12.2)	49(22.3)	77(35.0)
Total	92(41.8)	128(58.2)	220(100.0)

Chi-square : 1.45   Drgree of freedom : 2   Significant level : 0.48

* Figure shown in parenthesis refer to marginal percentage.

Table 6.2.4

B, Beta Weights Standard Error of 'B' Multipler, R, R Square and 'F' Ratio in Multiple Regression Analysis for Work—Related Variables as Significant Predictors of Quality of Working Life

Sr. No.	Variables	B	Beta Weight	Standard Error of B	Multipel R	R Square	F Ratio
1.	Tenure of Work Experience	−0.03	—0.00	0.20	0.35	0.12	0.02 NS
2.	No. of family members involved in construction work	—0.24	—0.03	0.27	0.35	0.12	0.74 NS
3.	Willingness to become Skilled Worker	—1.36	—0.09	0.49	0.39	0.15	7.60**
4.	Cooperation from Co-workers	0.62	0.06	0.35	0.43	0.18	3.14 NS
5.	Cooperation from Supervisor	—0.17	—0.01	0.37	0.43	0.18	0.22 NS
6.	Satisfaction from own work	0.44	0.03	0.57	0.30	0.92	0.59 NS
7.	Satisfaction from huaband's occupation	—0.10	—0.00	0.45	0.31	0.09	0.04 NS
8.	Satisfaction from Income	—0.74	—0.06	0.43	0.35	0.12	2.97 NS

**Significant at .01 level. NS: Not significant.

It is evident from the finding that the meaning of work experience has no value for women construction workers, because they have to every time move to different construction sites in search of work and because the occupations meant for them are only unskilled which do not require experience. In case of managerial level workers, Mishra (1985) also found that experience was not significantly related to QWL. The present set of findings are in tune with Mishra's findings.

Sub-hypothesis, in the context of women construction workers is therefore, accepted.

(*b*) *Number of Family Members Involved in Construction work*

As shown in Table 6.2.5 that the value of product moment correlation computed to determine relationship between number of family members involved in construction work and QWL, was found to be —0.030, which was not significant (Table 6.2.8). The value therefore, suggested that there was no relationship between the two variables.

The Chi-square value was also found in significant between high and low groups of QWL and number of family members involved in construction work (Table 6.2.5).

The multiple regression analysis was also run to know if number of family members involved in construction was a significant predictor of QWL. The 'F' ratio was found to be 0.74 which was found significant (Table 6.2.4).

Other family members if are involved with the same construction, work, provide psychological satisfaction and feeling of security. The women workers may in that case be more productive and may concentrate on job more efficiently enhancing QWL. But it seems that this factor does not affect QWL. It may, therefore, be said that the sub-hypothesis is accepted.

(*c*) *Willingness to become Skilled Worker*

The relationship between willingness to become skilled

Table 6.2.5

***Bivariate Frequency Distribution of Respondents Classified in Terms of Total Number of Family Members Involved in Construction Work and Quality of Working life**

Variable	*Quality of Working Life*		*Total*
Number of family members involved in construction work	*High (Score 35 and above)*	*Low (Score below 35)*	
Only one	13(5.9)	9(4.1)	22(10.0)
Two only	49(22.3)	76(34.5)	125(56.8)
Three only	15(6.8)	23(10.5)	38(17.3)
Four and more	15(6.8)	20(9.1)	35(15.9)
Total	92(41.8)	128(58.2)	220(100.0)

Chi-square : 3.15 Degree of freedom : 3 Significance level : 0.37

*Figures shown in parenthesis refer to marginal percentage.

worker with QWL was examined by computing product moment correlation. The value of correlation coefficient (9.228) suggested that the relation between the two variables was significant at0 .01 level (Table 6.2.2).

The value of the Chi-square was found to be 7.76 which was insignificant. This suggested that there was no significant difference between workers with high and low QWL and their willingness to become skilled workers. (Table 6.2.6).

The multiple regression analysis was also run to examine if willingness to become skilled worker was the predictor variable of QWL. The 'F' ratio suggested that willingness to become skilled worker was the predictor variable of QWL (7.60 significant at 0.01 level) as shown in Table 6.2.4.

Table 6.2.6

***Bivariate Frequency Distribution of Respondents Classified in Terms of their Willingness to become Skilled Workers and Quality of Working Life**

Willingness to become skilled worker	*Quality of Working Life*		*Total*
	High (Score 35 and above)	*Low (Score below 35)*	
Willing to become	73 (33.2)	119 (54.1)	192 (87.3)
Not willing to become	19 (8.6)	9 (4.1)	28 (12.7)
Total	92 (41.8)	128 (58.2)	220 (100.0)

Chi-square: 7.76 Degree of freedom: 1 Significant level: 0.005

*Figures shown in parenthesis refer to marginal percentage.

The percentage analysis reported in Appendix (Table 1.18) indicated that about 87.3 per cent of the workers were willing to become skilled for various reasons. Only 12.7 per cent responded were not interested to become a skilled worker. The skilled work has a high social and economic status in the society of construction workers. The status of skilled worker is one of the strong aspirations of women construction workers as it yields more wages which they see is earned by their male co-workers.

It may, therefore, be said that willingness to become skilled worker has relationship with QWL which means that the sub hypothesis is rejected.

(*d*) *Cooperation from Co-workers*

The relationship of cooperation from Co-workers and QWL was examined by computation of product moment correlation. The value obtained was 0.230 which was significant at 0.01 level. This is indicative of the fact that co-operation from co-workers had relationship with QWL (Table 6.2.2).

The multiple regression analysis also suggested that cooperation from co-workers was not a significant predictor of QWL as the 'F' ratio was found insignificant.

Cooperation from co-workers helps in increasing self-confidence and improvement of work quality. In case of women workers, it is further more useful as women tend to show immediate forming of association with co-workers. Joseph (1978) found in a study that co-workers have the potential to change QWL. The analysis, therefore, suggested that the sub-hypothesis is rejected but cannot be considered as predictor of QWL.

(*e*) *Cooperation from Supervisor*

The correlation coefficient of product moment correlation computed to examine relationship of QWL with cooperation from supervisor was found to be 0.139 which was not significant at 0.05 level. Hence, it may be said that this variable has no relation with QWL.

In the multiple regression analysis also the 'F' ratios showed that cooperation from supervisor had been found non-predictor of QWL (Table 6.2.4).

The study conducted by Joseph (1978) revealed that supervision and pay appear to be least associated with QWL. Mehta (1976) while studying higher level workers found that supervisory behaviours are important factors in work relaled satisfaction.

The sub-hypothesis is, therefore, accepted.

(*f*) *Satisfaction from Own Work*

The value of the coefficient of correlation (—0.015) indicated that this variable has no significant relation with QWL. To examine this relationship product moment correlation was computed (Table 6.2.2).

The value of Chi-square obtained was 0.33 which was not significant. This means that women workers in high and low QWL groups were equally satisfied as well as not satisfied with their own work. (Table 6.2.7).

The multiple regression analysis showed that the 'F' value (0.59) was not significant which means that satisfaction from own work was not predictor variable of QWL.

Table 6.2.7

***Bivarate Frequency Distribution of Respondents Classified in Terms of their Satisfaction from Own Work and Quality of Working Life**

Variable	*Quality of Working Life*		*Total*
Satisfaction from own work	*High (Score 35 and above)*	*Low (Score below 35)*	
Satisfied	15 (6.8)	26 (11.8)	41 (18.6)
Not Satisfied	77 (35.0)	102 (46.4)	179 (81.4)
Total	92 (41.8)	128 (58 2)	220 (100.0)

Chi-square : 0.33 Degree of freedom : 1 Significance level: 0.56

*Figures shown in the parenthesis refer to marginal percentage.

The sub-hypothesis is, therefore, accepted.

(g) *Satisfaction from Husband's Occupation*

For this variable also, product moment correlation with QWL was computed. The value of the coefficient of correlation was found to be —0.035 which was insignificant. This shows that no relationship existed between satisfaction from husband's occupation and QWL (Table 6.2.2).

The value of Chi-square was found to be 0.002 which was insignificant at 0.05 level. It may, therefore, be said that in both high and low groups on QWL of women workers, the feeling of satisfaction from husband's occupation was expressed equally (Table 6.2.8).

The multiple regression analysis showed that 'F' value (0.04) was not significant. Hence, satisfaction from husband's occupation was not predictor variable of QWL.

Table 6.2.8

***Bivariate Frequency Distribution of Respondents Classified in Terms of Satisfaction from Husband's Occupation and Quality of Working Life**

Variable	*Quality of Working Life*		*Total*
Satisfaction from husband's occupation	*High (Score 35 and above)*	*Low (Score below 35)*	
Satisfied	22 (11.2)	31 (15.8)	53 (27.0)
Not satisfied	58 (29.6)	85 (43.4)	143 (73.0)
Total	80 (40.8)	116 (59.2)	196 (100.0)

Chi-square : 0.002 Degree of Freedom : 1 Significance level : .97

*Figures shown in parenthesis refer to marginal percentage.

It may be because of the fact that husbands largely perform unskilled work with which the women workers felt dissatisfied.

In lieu of the above finding, it may be said that sub-hypothesis is accepted.

(*h*) *Satisfaction from Income*

The product moment correlation computed to examine relationship of QWL with this variable gave 0.131 as the value of the coefficient of correlation. This value was found insignificant at 0.05 level. Hence, it may be said that the variable did not have any relationship with QWL (Table 6.2.2).

The value of Chi-square was found to be 1.97 which was insignificant. It implied that both high and low QWL groups of workers equally felt satisfied as well as dissatisfied with their income (Table 6.2.9).

The multiple regression analysis indicated that satisfaction from income was not the predictor variable of QWL as the value of 'F' ratio was found to be insignificant (2.97).

Table 6.2.9

***Bivariate Frequency Distribution of Respondents Classified in Terms of their Satisfaction from Income and Quality of Working Life**

Variable / *Satisfaction from Income*	*Quality of Working Life* *High* *(Score 35 and above)*	*Low* *(Score below 35)*	*Total*
Satisfied	26 (11.8)	49 (22.3)	75 (34.1)
Not satisfied	66 (30.0)	79 (35.9)	145 (65.9)
Total	92 (41.8)	128 (58.2)	220 (100.0)

Chi-square : 1.97 Degree of freedom : 1 Significance level : 0.16

*Figures shown in parenthesis refer to marginal percentage.

The results may be compared with some of the findings which stated that income satisfaction have association with QWL.

The sub-hypothesis is, therefore, accepted.

3. Relationship of Selected Living Condition Variables with QWL

The relationship of living condition variables with QWL was examined by computation of product moment correlation. In case of living condition variables only two variables were examined in details, the housing facility rating and hours of rest. Both of these were considered most important as they refer to two important necessities of living conditions. The inter-correlation among living condition variables are given in Table 6.3.1.

Hypothesis III

The hypothesis indicated that living condition variables will not have any relationship with QWL and the variables tested were considered as sub-hypotheses.

(*a*) *Housing Facility Rating*

The housing facility rating was obtained on a three

Table 6.3.1

Introduction among Selected Living Condition Variables

Sr. No.	*Living Condition Variables*	*1*	*2*	*3*	*4*	*5*	*6*	*7*	*8*	*9*	*10*	*11*
1.	Living Space Provided	1	—01	07	—03	08	—04	—04	—04	—27**	11	—04
2.	Description of 'Jhuggi'		1	—02	19*	08	—10	11	12	02	—08	01
3.	Housing Facility Rating			1	—17*	—14	—06	11	—05	—16*	06	00
4.	*Availability of: Street Light*				1	48**	08	20*	19	03	—16*	—06
5.	Pavements					1	02	13	18	04	—08	—07
6.	Community Toilets						1	03	13	—05	—18*	12
7.	Medical Centre							1	14	10	—03	—08
8.	Cleaning Services								1	09	—17*	00
9.	Ration Card									1	—11	03
10.	Child Care Centre										1	03
11.	Hours of Rest											1

p ◁ .05 r=0.161 *Significant at .05 level. **Significant at .01 level.

p ◁ .01 r=0.211 All decimals have been removed other than diagonals.

point scale and the score obtained were correlated with QWL. The product moment correlation was computed and the value of coefficient of correlation obtained was 0.031, which was found insignificant at 0.05 level. This indicated that housing facility provided to women workers has no relationship with their perception of QWL.

(*b*) *Hours of Rest*

The relationship of hours of rest and QWL was determined by computation of product moment correlation. The value of coefficient of correlation was found to be 0.074 which was insignificant. This means that there was no relation between QWL and hours of rest.

The multiple regression analysis also showed that both housing facility rating and hours of rest do not contribute as predictors of QWL.

It may therefore, be said that the sub-hypothesis is accepted and inall, hypothesis III is accepted.

4. Relationship of General Awareness with QWL

To study the relationship between General Awareness of the women construction workers with QWL, Pearson's Product Moment Correlation was determined. The student 't' statistics were also computed to determine the significant difference between the two mean scores of the respondents on General Awareness in relation to their level of QWL.

Hypothesis IV

The hypothesis stated that general awarness of the women construction workers has no relationship with QWL.

The Product Moment Correlation was computed to examine relationship between general awareness of the women construction workers with QWL. The value obtained was 0.108 which was not significant even at 0.05 level.The value indicated that there is no relationship between general awareness and QWL.

In order to determine whether general awareness of the women workers differ significantly with respect to the mean scores on QWL questionnaire, student 't' statistics was used. The figures are indicated in Table 6.4.1.

Table 6.4.1

Results of 't' Statistics between High and Low QWL with General Awareness of the Respondents

Variable	*Mean*		*SD*		*SE*		*DF*	*'t' Ratio*
	High QWL	*Low QWL*	*High QWL*	*Low QWL*	*High QWL*	*Low QWL*		
General Awareness	14.4	15.0	2.19	2.51	0.23	0.22	218	—2.03*

*Significant at 3.05 level.

The 't' value was found to be —2.03 which was significant at .05 level. This indicated that General Awareness was significantly different with QWL levels. It may, therefore, be said that hypothesis IV is rejected.

5. Relationship of Attiiude Towards Education with QWL

The attitude towards education of the women workers was obtained on a three point scale and an aggregate score was derived. The relationship of attitude towards education with QWL was determined by computation of product moment correlation. The students' 't' statistics was also computed to find out, if there existed significant difference between the mean scoresof the attitude towards education in relation to level of QWL of the women workers.

Hypothesis V

The hypothesis stated that attitude towards education of the women workers has no *relationship* with QWL.

The product moment correlation was computed to examine relationship of attitude towards education of the respondents with QWL. They computed value of the correlation coefficient was 0.115 which was not significant at 0.05 level. This indicated that both attitude towards education and QWL were not associated with each other.

In order to examine whether attitude towards education of the women workers, significantly differed with respect to mean scores on QWL, student 't' statistics was computed. The figure obtained are given in Table 6.5.1.

Table 6.5.1

Results of 't' Statistics between High and Low QWL with Attitude towards Education of the Respondents

Variable	*Mean*		*SD*		*SE*		*DF*	*Ratio*
	High QWL	*Low QWL*	*High QWL*	*Low QWL*	*High QWL*	*Low QWL*		
Attitude towards Education	22.8	23.3	2.56	2.95	0.27		218	—1.21 NS

NS—Not significant.

The value of 't' Ratio (—1.21) indicated that there was no sisuificant difference between QWL and attitude towards education of the women workers. The mean score also indicated that the difference was very small. Therefore, hypothesis V is accepted.

6. Relationship of Performance Level with RWL

To find out the relationship between the performance level with QWL, product moment correlation was computed for each of the dimensions of the performance level. The multiple regression and step wise regression was also worked out. The Correlation among various dimensions is presented in Table 6.6.1.

Table 6.6.1

Intercorrelation Among Various Dimensions of Performance Level Assessment

Sr. No.	Performance Level Dimensions	1	2	3	4	5	6	7	8	9	10	11	12	13	14	15
1.	Physical Strength	1	42**	39**	46**	41**	41**	40**	35**	38**	36**	38**	39**	48**	60**	56**
2.	Daily Out put		1	28**	25**	39**	37**	31**	32**	37**	29**	27**	29**	34**	51**	54**
3.	Perfection in Work			1	47**	34**	36**	25**	38**	43**	21**	34**	37**	43**	61**	63**
4.	Quality of work				1	40**	29**	30**	35**	37**	37**	46**	38**	44**	57**	55**
5.	Obedience					1	44**	30**	26**	36**	31**	30**	38**	46**	51**	57**
6.	Regularity of Work						1	41**	24**	36**	28**	28**	38**	45**	56**	57**
7.	Understanding the Job							1	40**	31**	19**	16*	30**	39**	52**	51**
8.	Coordination of Work								1	50**	17**	27**	33**	34**	51**	51**
9.	Relation with Co-workers									1	46**	38**	31**	42**	60**	56**
10.	Relation with Supervisor										1	54**	22**	39**	51**	48**
11.	Overcoming Problems Independently											1	38**	32**	55**	53**
12.	Learning New Works												1	46**	57**	52**
13.	Interest in Work													1	63**	65**
14.	Overall Performance														1	81**
15.	Total Performance															1

$p<0.05$ $r=0.161$ *Significant at 0.05 level. **Significant at 0.01 level.

$p\triangleleft 0.01$ $r-0.211$ Decimal have been removed in all columns other than diagonals.

Hypothesis VI

The hypothesis stated that performance level of the women workers will not be significantly related to QWL.

As stated earlier, performance level was assessed by the immediate supervisors of the women workers on a five point scale. An attempt was made to find out relationship of all the 14 dimensions of the performance level assessment with QWL. The relationship was examined by computation of product moment correlation. The correlation coefficients obtained for each dimension is mentioned in Table 6.6.2.

Table 6.6.2

Intercorrelations between Dimensions of Performance level Assessment and QWL

Sr. No.	*Performance Dimensions*	*'r' with QWL*
1.	Physical Strength	0.719**
2.	Daily Out put	0.537**
3.	Performance in Work	0.556**
4.	Quality of Work	0.546**
5.	Obedience	0.487**
6.	Regularity of Work	0.470**
7.	Understanding the Job	0.465**
8.	Coordination of Work	0.512**
9.	Relation with Co-workers	0.554**
10.	Relation with Supervisor	0.493**
11.	Overcoming Problems Independently	0.577**
12.	Learning of new works	0.476**
13.	Interest in Work	0.604**
14.	Overall Performance	0.732**

**Significant at 0.01 level.

It is evident from the Table 6.6.2 that the dimensions of the performance level assessment were found significantly correlated with QWL. The value of the coefficient of correlation was in all cases more than 0.450.

To test the hypothesis which stated that dimensions of performance level assessment were not the significant predictors of QWL, multiple regression was run as presented in Table 6.6.3.

Table 6.6.3

B, Beta Weight, Standard Error of 'B', Multiple R, 'R' Square and 'F' Ratio in Multiple Regression Analysis for Dimensions of Performance Level Assessment as Significant Predictors of QWL

Sr. No.	*Variable*	*B*	*Beta weight*	*Standard Error of B*	*Multiple R*	*R Square*	*F Ratio*
1.	Physical Strength	1.11	0.21	0.21	0.76	0.58	25.84**
2.	Daily out-put	0.54	0.11	0.17	0.81	0.66	9.26**
3.	Perfection in Work	0.71	0.14	0.19	0.85	0.73	13.59**
4.	Quality of Work	0.10	0.02	0.19	0.87	0.75	0.30 NS
5.	Obedience	0.19	0.04	0.18	0.87	0.76	1.18 NS
6.	Regularity of Work	0.15	0.03	0.18	0.87	0.76	0.73 NS
7.	Understanding of Work	0.46	0.09	0.17	0.88	0.77	6.72**
8.	Coordination of Work	0.31	0.07	0.17	0.88	0.78	3.27 NS
9.	Relation with Co-worker	0.26	0.06	0.17	0.89	0.79	2.21 NS
10.	Relation with Supervisor	—0.03	0.00	0.19	0.89	0.80	0.02 NS
11.	Overcoming Problems Independently	0.89	0.20	0.18	0.90	0.82	23.83**
12.	Learning of New work	0.09	0.02	0.16	0.90	0.82	0.33 NS
13.	Interest in work	0.32	0.06	0.19	0.91	0.82	0.74 NS
14.	Overall Performance	—0.82	—0.12	0.45	0.91	0.82	3.23 NS

**Significant at 0.01 level NS—Not Significant

The multiple regression analysis showed that out of 14 dimensions of performance level assessment, only five variables have been found as predictor variables of QWL, they were physical strength, daily out-put, perfection in work, understanding of work and overcoming problems independently. The obtained value of 'F' ratios were significant at 0.01 level. These variables accounting for 80 per cent of total variance which is statistically significant in predicting QWL.

Quality of work, obedience, regularity of work, relation with co-workers, relation with supervisor, overall performance and interest in work seemed to have negligible predictive capacity. All the 14 dimensions in equation accounted for 82 per cent of variance.

It may, therefore, be said that the hypothesis gets partial support. Only five dimensions have been found significant predictors whereas, rest nine dimensions do not predict QWL.

7. Relationsbip of Need Fulfilment with QWL

To find out the relationship between the need hierarchy, i.e., basic needs, security needs, belonging needs, esteem needs and self actualization with QWL, product moment correlations were computed. The multiple regression and step-wise multiple regression were also worked out. The correlation among the five needs is presented in Table 6.7.1.

Hypothesis VII

The hyyothesis stated that need fulfilment has no relationship with QWL.

In order to test the aforesaid hypothesis product moment correlation of the need hierarchy with QWL was computed. The correlation coefficients have been presented in Table 6.7.2.

Table 6.7.1

Intercorrelations among Hierarchy Needs

Sr. No.	*Hierarchy Needs*	*1*	*2*	*3*	*4*	*5*
1.	Basic Needs	1	38**	33**	33**	31**
2.	Security Needs		1	43**	45**	49**
3.	Belonging Needs			1	46**	54**
4.	Esteem Needs				1	70**
5.	Self Actualization Needs					1

$p < 0.01$ $r = 0.211$ **Significant at 0.01 level.

Decimals have been removed other than diagonals.

Table 6.7.2

Intercorrelations between Hierarchy of Needs and QWL

Sr. No.	*Hierarchy Needs*	*'r' with QWL*
1.	Basic Needs	0.503**
2.	Security Needs	0.636**
3.	Belonging Needs	0.624**
4.	Esteem Needs	0.673**
5.	Self Actualization Needs	0.664**

**Significant at .01 level.

As evident from the above Table that all the needs of the hierarchy are related to QWL. The women workers look forward to basic needs (0.503), security needs (0.636), belonging needs (0.624), esteem needs (0.673) and self actualization needs (0.664) in relation to the perception of QWL.

The multiple regression analysis was also run to test the hypothesis VII. A stepwise multiple regression analysis of need hierarchy was performed to derive significant predictors of QWL, amongst the five need variables. The computed results of multiple regression analysis can be seen from Table 6.7.3.

Table 6.7.3

B, Beta weight, Standard Error of 'B', Multiple R, R Square and 'F' Ratio in Multiple Regression Analysis for Need Hierarchy as Predictors of QWL

Sr. No.	*Variable*	*B*	*Belta weight*	*Standard Error of B*	*Multiple R*	*R Square*	*R Ratio*
1.	Basic needs	1.08	0.11	0.32	0.92	0.84	10.94**
2.	Security needs	0.91	0.11	0.31	0.92	0.85	8.60**
3.	Belonging needs	0.82	0.11	0.27	0.93	0.86	8.86**
4.	Esteem needs	1.12	0.17	0.33	0.93	0.87	13.23**
5.	Self Actualization	—0.51	—0.07	0.34	0.93	0.87	2.26NS

NS: Not Significant **Significant at 0.01 level

The variables that were found significant predictors of QWL and significant at 0.01 level were basic needs, security needs, needs of belongingness and esteem needs. These four need variables accounted for 86 percent of the total variance. It means these four variables are significant predictors of QWL. The remaining only one, self actualization needs seemed to have negligible predictive capacity. All the five variables in equation account for 87 per cent of total variance. Results further revealed that self-actualization was not related to QWL.

The hypothesis was further tested by computation of 't' statistics. The results indicated that in both high and low QWL groups, determined on the basis of median value (35), the respondents were significantly different on need hierarchy. All the values of 't' ratio showed a minus sign which indicated that higher the need satisfaction, higher will be the QWL (Table 6.7.4).

Table 6.7.4

Results of 't' Statistics between High and Low QWL with Need Hierarchy Variables

Sr. No.	*Variable*	*Mean*		*S.D.*		*S.E.*		*DF*	*'t' Ratio*
		High	*Low*	*High*	*Low*	*High*	*Low*		
1.	Basic needs	2.72	3.19	0.55	0.41	0.06	0.04	218	−6.81**
2.	Security needs	1.83	2.48	0.59	0.50	0.06	0.04	218	−8.58**
3.	Belonging needs	1.35	1.98	0.62	0.68	0.06	0.06	218	−7.18**
4.	Esteem need	0.85	1.59	0.46	0.68	0.05	0.06	218	−9.57**
5.	Self actualization	0.64	1.28	0.29	0.85	0.03	0.07	218	−9.19**

**Significant at .01 level.

The construction women workers tend to look forward to the satisfaction of all types of needs and self actualization to some degree is not proved as predictor variables of QWL. The opportunity to show excellence is rather low in the unskilled occupation. The realization of basic needs is predominant at every stage of the work activity. Mehra (1984) in his study found that need fulfilment of the subjects was highly correlated with income and length of service, whereas Mishra (1985) found that need fulfilment was the deciding factor in QWL perception of employees.

In view of the findings, it may be stated that hypothesis VII is partially accepted.

Summary of the Findings

In the context of relevant research literature on QWL among women construction workers, seven null hypothese were framed with regard to all the variables under study such as background variables, work related variables, living condition variables, general awareness, attitude towards education, performance level, and need fulfilment.

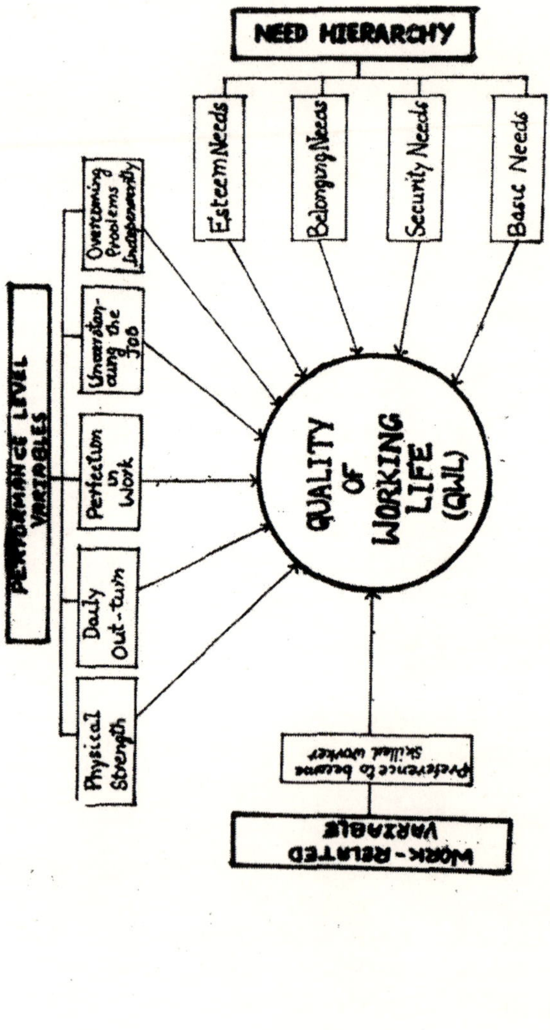

A PROPOSED MODEL OF QWL OF WOMEN CONSTRUCTION WORKERS

Out of the nine selected background variables only three were found significantly related to QWL, such as, migration category, educational status and per capita monthly family income of the respondents. None of the variables were found as significant predictors of QWL.

None of the living condition variables were related to QWL.

The general awareness was found not related to QWL but the high and low group on QWL significantly differed with each other. It was also not found as significant predictor of QWL.

The attitude towards education was also not significantly related to QWL and the high and low levels of QWL did not differ significantly.

All the fourteen dimensions of performance level assessment were found significantly related to QWL, however, only five dimensions were found predictors of QWL such as physical strength, daily out-put, perfection in work, understanding of work and overcoming problems independently.

The need hierarchy i.e. basic, security, belonging, esteem and self-actualization needs were found significantly related to QWL. Only self-actualization was not found as predictor variable of QWL, otherwise all the four needs showed their significant predictive capacity.

7

Implications and Suggestions

Implication of the Study

The present study has highlighted certain basic feature of the quality of working life of the women construction workers in the construction industry which reflected shortfalls of this unorganized sector of industry. At presant in the country labour laws have provided insufficient rights to women in the construction industry, the protection of these rights must be exercised with great care and control. The women workers do not have adequate exposure to educational opportunities but they understand the meaning and benefits of education. The present investigation has found that the women construction workers have high scores on attitude towards education. The educational planners must devise an appropriate method to provide educational facilities to the construction workers so as to impart vocational training which will facilitate development of skills required in the construction industry. Special emphasis must be laid down on skill development training to women and their needs. Efforts should also be made to provide educational opportunities to the children of these workers.

It is obvious from the study that women remain in exploitative situation in the construction industry. The dual role conflict of working as well as child rearing creates constant mental stress and divided attention. As a result of this the performance level of these workers is estimated quite low. At the work sites child care centres should be available. The undivided attention of these workers will bring about better performance and productivity, thereby rising the quality of working life.

The study also revealed the fact that in spite of constant problem of new job searching and sub-standard living and working conditions, women workers look forward to satisfaction of their basic needs and also higher order needs to evolve a respectable image in the society. If adequat e attempts are made to satisfy the lower order needs, there would be enhancement in productivity and the satisfaction of higher order needs will be an automatic process. The economic gains of better productivity will lead to betterquality of working life.Attempts should also be made to prepare women workers to accept higher occupations (of skilled workers) in the construction industry for earning more wages and becoming economically stronger.

The basic facilities such as food, shelter and housing should be made available easily to these workers who are already economically deprived and are unaware of the urban life. The insecurity and instability of employment is a policy issue. The attention to it is necessary because it directly affects the quality of working life of the workers in the construction industry. The condition of organised sector was not so organised as they are today in the pre-independence and early years of independence. The attention was paid immediately as they were vital to contribute substantially to the economy of the country. Construction industry remained un-noticed for long. Now the times has come when the country is marching ahead in the 21st century, the unorganised sector should also acquire organised form and the workers should be given equal opportunity to improve their life as a whole and the quality of working life in particular.

Limitations of the Study

—The study was limited to women workers involved with construction agencies operating in Delhi only.

—The study reflected QWL observations of a particular time period only and it could have been more revealing if it could have been conducted at different times to study any change in QWL of women construction workers.

—A number of variables which may probably have relationship with QWL could not be studied due to non-availability of literature as well as standard instruments for measurement of such variables. The time limit also did not permit construction of instruments suited to illiterate women construction workers.

—A comparative study of other category of workers in the unorganised sector such as agriculture, domestic spheres, petty trades etc. would have also provided strength to the present investigation.

The study also offers suggestions for further research in two directions, which are as fo'lows:

Suggestions Regarding Action Oriented Research:

1. Improvement of the quality of working life in the context of women construction workers is not only a research topic but lot of action is needed to be taken. Research based feed-back actions must be planned to impart vocational education for the development of appropriate skills.

2. Detailed studies must be undertaken to identify skill status of the women workers.

3. Documentation of the personal profile of the workers must be maintained by some employment agency so that for future employment the workers refer to this agency and immediate employment is granted to them,

4. All concepts leading to productivity should also be applied and tested on workers belonging to lower cadres in the organised sector. Research should be conducted to evolve a strategy to organise construction industry. The result of such studies should be immediately implemented and on the basis of their effects on improvement of quality of working life should be studied.

Suggestions Pegarding Scope of Psychological Researches:

5. Psychological parametres have a potential role to play in the studies analysing cause and effect relationships. In case of QWL the importance of psychological parametres should be studied thoroughly. Many work conditions have psychological feelings which may be different in case of individual worker. Such parametres need further research.

6. Ergonomical studies also have importance in the construction industry which will throw light on initial level of skill development among the entrants in the construction labour market and also to study the progressive development of skills in due course of time.

7. The sample size taken for the present study was quite small as compared to the total universe of women construction workers. The study confined to women workers in Delhi only. More comprehensive studies with large sample size on all India basis, must be conducted.

8. Due to certain practical difficulties, the present study could not include some of the important variables which probably could have been more useful to determine relationship with quality of working life of women construction workers. Future studies in this area should take care of these variables.

9. Certain enquiries, such as, family planning practices, physical harassment of women, grievances against employer etc. were not included in the present investigation because they are themselves research areas for psychologists.
10. In the present study construction of research instruments was almost an independent exercise. There are almost negligible efforts so far made to develop research instruments for illiterate workers. Research should be undertaken to develop such instruments.

Apart from psychological researches, interdisciplinary researches have urgent need. It is true also in today's world that interaction of technology and human approach have to marry together to arrive at accepted system of life.

Appendix

Percentage Analysis Tables

Table 1.1

Percentage and Frequency Distribution of Age of the Respondents

Age Group	*Frequency*	*Percentage*
Upto 15 years	11	5.0
16-20 years	26	11.8
21-25 years	64	29.1
26-30 years	50	22.8
31-35 years	15	6.8
36-40 years	30	13.6
41-45 years	16	7.3
Above 45 years	8	3.6
		100.0
Total		(220)

Table 1.2

Percentage and Frequency Distribution of Caste of the Respondents

Caste	*Frequency*	*Percentage*
Scheduled Castes	114	51.8
Scheduled Tribes	18	8.2
Others	88	40.0
		100.0
Total		(220)

Table 1.3

Percentage and Frequency Distribution of Religion of the Respondents

Religion	*Frequency*	*Percentage*
Hindu	211	95.9
Muslim	9	4.1
		100.0
Total		(220)

Table 1.4

Percentage and the Frequency Distribution of the Marital Status of the Respondents

Material Status	*Frequency*	*Percentage*
Married	201	91.4
Unmarried	13	5.9
Divorced	2	0.9
Widow	4	1.8
		100.0
Total		(220)

Table 1.5

Percentage and Frequency Distribution of the Respondents by Migration Category

Migration Category	*Frequency*	*Percentage*
Permanent migrants	71	32.3
Seasonal migrants	149	67.7
		100.0
Total		(220)

Table 1.6

Percentage and Frequency Distribution of the Educational Status of the Respondents

Educational Status	*Frequency*	*Percentage*
Illiterate	204	92.7
Upto 3rd standard	12	5.5
Upto 5th standard	2	0.9
Above 5th standard	2	0.9
		100.0
Total		(220)

Table 1.7

Percentage and Frequency Distribution of type of the Family and the Respondents

Family Type	*Frequency*	*Percentage*
Nuelear	154	70.0
Joint	66	30.0
		100.0
Total		(220)

Table 1.8

Percentage and Frequency Distribution of the Size of the Family of the Respondents

Family Size	*Frequency*	*Percentage*
Two	27	12.3
Three	44	20.0
Four	68	30.9
Five	47	21.4
Six	21	9.5
Seven	10	4.5
Eight	3	1.4
		100.0
Total		(220)

Table 1.9

Percentage ond Frequency Distribution of Respondents and Occupation of their Husbands

Husband's Occupation	*Frequency*	*Percentage*
Unskilled worker	154	70.0
Skilled worker	37	16.8
Absent/Does not contribute to the family income	29	13.2
		100.0
Total		(220)

Table 1.10

Percentage and Frequency Distribution of Average Age of the Family Members

Average Family Age	*Frequency*	*Percentage*
15 to 19 years	82	37.3
20 to 24 years	60	27.3
25 to 29 years	47	21.3
30 years and above	31	14.1
		100.0
Total		(220)

Table 1.11

Percentage and Frequency Distribution of Average Education of the Family Members

Average Family Education	*Frequency*	*Percentage*
Illiterate	171	77.7
Upto 3re standard	40	18.1
Upto 5th standard	7	3.2
8th standard and above	2	1.0
		100.0
Total		(220)

Table 1.12

Percentage and Frequency Distribution of Per Capita Monthly Family Income of the Respondents

Per Capita Monthly Family Income	*Frequency*	*Percentage*
Upto Rs. 50	5	2.3
Rs. 51 to Rs. 100	30	13.6
Rs. 101 to 200	107	48.6
Rs. 201 to Rs. 300	59	26.8
Rs. 301 to Rs. 400	14	6.4
Above Rs. 400	5	2.3
		100.0
Total		(220)

Table 1.13

Percentage and Frequency Distribuion of the Respondents by Tenure of Work Experience

Tenure of Work Experience	*Frequency*	*Percentage*
Upto 1 year	60	27.3
2 years	32	14.5
3 years	37	16.8
4 years	14	6.4
5 years	19	8.6
6 years	9	4.1
7 years	9	4.1
8 and more years	40	18.2
		100.0
Total		(220)

Table 1.14

Percentage and Frequency Distribution of the Respondents by Working Status

working status	*Frequeney*	*Perceatage*
Full time	81	36.8
Part time	105	37.7
Work available for less than 25 days in a month	34	15.5
		100.0
Total		(220)

Table 1.15

Percentage and Frequency Distribution of the Respondents by Number of Family Members involved in Construction Work

Number of family members involved in construction work	*Frequency*	*Percentage*
One	22	10.1
Two	125	56.8
Three	38	17.3
Four	30	13.6
Five	5	2.3
		100.0
Total		(220)

Table 1.16

Percentage and Frequency Distribution of Skilled Construction Works Liked by the Respondents

Skilled construction Works liked	*Frequency*	*Percentage*
Masonary	102	46.4
Carpentry	7	3.2
Electrician	5	2.3
None of these	69	41.4
Any other	47	16.4
		100.0
Total		(220)

Table 1.17

Percentage and Frequency Distribution of Respondents by Out of Construction Work Skills Liked

Out of Construction Work Skills Liked	*Frequency*	*Percentage*
Knitting	9	4.1
Embroidery	11	5.0
Tailoring	73	33.2
Papad Making	2	0.9
Shop Keeping	7	3.2
Agriculture	50	22.7
None of these	53	24.1
Any other	15	6.8
		100.0
Total		(220)

Table 1.18

Percentage and Frequency Distribution of Willingness to Become Skilled Workers by the Respondents

Willingness to become Skilled Worker	*Frequency*	*Percentage*
Willing to become	192	87.3
Not wiling to become	28	12.7
		100.0
Total		(220)

Table 1.19

Percentage and Frequency Distribution of Respondents by the Reasons for not Becoming Skilled Worker

Reasons for not becoming a skilled worker	*Frequency*	*Percentage*
Lack of Physical Strength	9	4.1
Lack of Mental Ability	73	33.2
Social Problems	22	10.0
Husband's resistance	13	5.9
Lack of training opportunities	63	28.6
Any other	40	18.6
		100.0
Total		(220)

Table 1.20

Percentage and Frequency Distribution of Respondonts by Existing Skills Known

Existing Skills Known	*Frequency*	*Percentage*
Knitting	6	2.7
Embroidery	13	5.9
Tailoring	35	15.9
Papad Making	1	0.5
Shop Keeping	2	0.5
None of these	157	71.4
Any other	6	2.7
		100.0
Total		(220)

Table 1.21

Percentage and Frequency Distribution of Problems Faced by Dual Work Performing of the Respondents

Problem	*Frequency*	*Percentage*
Differences with husband	14	6.4
Differences with other family members	14	6.4
Negligence in child care	62	28.2
Neglience in household work	13	5.9
Absenteeism/late comer on work	1	0.5
Tiredness	98	44.5
Any other	18	8.2
		100.0
Total		(220)

Table 1.22

Percentage and Frequency Distribution of the Respondents by Condition of Equipment

Condition of Equipment	*Frequency*	*Percentage*
Good	41	18.6
Bad	48	21.8
Just Right	131	59.8
		100.0
Total		(220)

Table 1.23

Percentage and Frequency Distribution of the Respondents by Co-operation from their Co-workers

Cooperation from Co-workers available	*Frequency*	*Percentage*
Yes	105	47.7
No	115	52.3
		100.0
Total		(220)

Table 1.24

Percentage and Frequency Distribution of the Respondents by Availability of Co-operation from their Supervisor

Cooperation from Supervisor	*Frequency*	*Percentage*
Available	71	32.3
Not available	149	67.7
		100.0
Total		(220)

Table 1.25

Percentage and Preqnency Distribution of the Respondents Satisfaction from Own Work

Satisfaction from Own Work	*Frequency*	*Percentage*
Yes	41	18.6
No	179	81.4
		100.0
Total		(220)

Table 1.26

Percentnge and Frequency Distribution of Respondents by Satisfaction from Husband's Occupation

Satisfaction from Husband's occupation	*Frequency*	*Percentage*
Satisfied	53	24.1
Not satisfied	167	75.9
		100.0
Total		(220)

Table 1.27

Percentage and Frequency Distribution of Respondents by Satisfaction from Income

Satisfaction from Income	*Frequency*	*Percentage*
Yes	75	34.0
No	145	66.0
		100.0
Total		(220)

Table 1.28

Percentage and Frequeney Distribution of Respondents by the Living Space Provided by

Living Space Provided by	*Frequency*	*Percentage*
Middle man	66	30.0
Contractor	91	41.4
Self Occupied	52	23.6
Any other	11	5.0
		100.0
Total		(220)

Table 1.29

Percentage and Frequency Distribution of Respondents by Discription of the Hutment

Discription of ihe Hutment	*Frequency*	*Percentage*
Kachcha without electricity, water supply and bathroom	200	90.9
Kachcha with electricity, water supply and bathroom	6	2.7
Pukka without electricity, water supply and bathroom	10	4.5
Pukka with electricity, water supply and bathroom	4	1.8
		100.0
Total		(220)

Table 1.30
Percentage and Frequency Distribution of Respondents by Housing Facility Rating

Housing Facility	*Frequency*	*Percentage*
Good	6	2.7
So So	137	62.3
Not at all Good	77	35.0
		100.0
Total		(220)

Table 1.31
Percentage and Frequency Distribution of the Respondents by Public Utilities Availability

Public Utility Availability	*Frequency*		*Percentage*		
	Yes	*No*	*Yes*	*No*	
Street Light	106	114	48.2	51.8	100.0
Pavements	105	115	47.7	42.2	100.0
Medical Centre	35	185	15.0	81.1	100.0
Community Toilets	50	170	22.7	77.3	100.0
Cleaning Services	52	168	23.6	76.4	100.0
Ration Card	53	167	24.1	75.9	100.0
Child Care Centre	89	151	31.4	68.6	100.0
Total					(220)

Table 1.32

Percentage and Frequency Distribution and Mean Scores of Various Dimensions of Performance Level Assessmen on Five Point Scale

Sr. No.	Performance Level Assessment	Very Good (5)	Good (4)	So so (3)	Bad (2)	Very Bad (1)	Total	Mean Score
	1	2	3	4	5	6	7	8
1.	Physical Strəngth	20 (9.1)	32 (14.5)	109 (49.6)	41 (18.7)	18 (8.1)	220 (100.0)	2.98
2.	Daily out-put	16 (7.2)	25 (11.3)	78 (35.5)	78 (35.5)	23 (10.5)	220 (100.0)	2.70
3.	Perfection in work	16 (7.2)	46 (21.0)	88 (40.0)	94 (21.3)	23 (10.5)	220 (100.0)	2.93
4.	Quality of work	14 (6.4)	62 (28.1)	78 (35.5)	48 (21.9)	18 (8 1)	220 (100.6)	3.02
5.	Obedience	16 (7.3)	54 (24.6)	72 (32.8)	60 (27.2)	18 (8.1)	220 (100.0)	2.95
6.	Regularity of work	17 (8.1)	44 (20.0)	78 (35.5)	57 (25.9)	23 (10.5)	220 (100.0)	2.90

(Contd.)

Table 1.32 (Contd.)

1	2	3	4	5	6	7	8
7. Understanding the job	15	42	70	66	27	220	2.78
	(6.9)	(19.1)	(31.8)	(30.0)	(12.2)	(100.0)	
8. Coordination of work	16	50	56	69	29	220	1.98
	(7.2)	(22.8)	(25.5)	(31.4)	(13.1)	(100.0)	
9. Relation with co-workers	21	52	70	42	35	220	2.92
	(9.5)	(23.7)	(31.9)	(19.4)	(15.9)	(100.0)	
10. Relation with Supervisor	12	57	64	69	24	220	2.81
	(5.5)	(23.2)	(29.0)	(31.4)	(10.9)	(100.0)	
11. Overcoming Problems Independently	22	42	58	74	24	220	2.84
	(10.0)	(19.1)	(26.3)	(33.2)	(10.9)	(100.0)	
12. Learning new work	19	46	61	67	27	220	2.83
	(8.7)	(20.9)	(27.8)	(30.4)	(12.2)	(100.0)	
13. Interest in work	34	44	91	39	12	220	3.22
	(15.4)	(20.0)	(41.3)	(17.8)	(5.5)	(100.0)	
14. Overall Performance	—	38	102	76	4	220	2.79
	—	(17.2)	(46.3)	(34.6)	(1.9)	(100.0)	

Figures in parenthesis are percentages.

Bibliography

Abrams, M. (1973) 'Subjective Social Indicators', *Social Trends*, No. 4. London : HMSO.

Adams, J.S. (1965) Injustice in Social Exchange. In L. Berkowitz (Ed.) *Advances in Experimental Social Psychology*, Vol. 2, New York : Free Press.

Aiken, M and Hage, J. (1966) Organizational Alienation : A comparative analysis, *American Sociological Review*, 31, 497-507.

Alderfer, C.P. (1969) 'An Empirical Test of a New Theory of Human Needs', *Organizational Behaviour and Human Performance*, Vol. 4, 142-75.

Alderfer, C.P. (1972) *Existance, Relatedness and Growth : Haman Needs in Organizational Settings*, New York, Free Press.

Andrew F. Sikula, John F. McKenna (1984) '*The Management of Human Resources*', Personnel Text and Current Issues, John Wiley and Sons, New York, 120-126.

Andrews, F.M. and S.B. Withey (1976) '*Social Indicators of Mell-Being*', New York : Plenum.

Anthony, W.P. (1978) '*Participative Management.*' Boston : Addison-Wesley.

Bergemaoer, R., Borg, I and Joseh, E. (1984) 'Structural Relationships among Facets of Work and General Well-being', *Psychological Abstracts*. Vol. 11(2), 163-181.

Blauner R. (1964) '*Alienation and Freedom.*' Chicago: University of Chicago Press.

Blishen, B and Atkinson, T. (1978) 'Anglophone and Francophone Differences in Perceptions of the Quality of Life in Canada'. *The Quality of Life—Comparative Studies*, (Ed.) Szalai, A. and Andrews, F.M., Sage Publication, California, 25-39.

Boisvert, M.P. (1977) *The Quality of Working Life: An Analysis: Human Relations*, 30(2), 155-160.

Bossely, H. (1976) '*Information Processing, Congnitive Dissonances and Basic Needs : The Modelling of Behaviour*', H. Bossel et.al. (Eds.), System Theory in the Social Sciences.

Bowers, D.G. and Franklin, J.L. (1977) '*Suney Guided Development : Data-based Organizational Change*', San Diego. C.A. : University Associates,

Bridges, F.J. and Chapmen, J.E. (1977) '*Critical Incidents in Organizational Behaviour and Administration*', Englewood Cliffs, N.J, : Prentice-Hall.

Bronowski, J. (1974) '*The Ascent of Man*', Boston : Little Brown, 448.

Campbell, J.P., Dunnetta, M.D , Lawler, E.E. III and Weick, K.E. (1970) '*Managerial Behaviour, Performance and Effectiveness*', New York : McGraw Hill.

Campbell, A., Converse. P.E. and Rodgers, W.L. (1976) '*The Quality of American Life*', New York : Russell Sage.

Carlson, C. (1977) 'A Model of Quality of Work Life as a Developmental Process.' *Education and Training*, January, 27-32,

Cherns, A. (1975) 'Perspectives on the Quality of Working Life, *Journal of Occupational Psychology*, 48, 153-167.

Cherns, A.B. (1973) 'Belter Wasking Lives; A Social Scientists View', *Journal of Occupational Psychology*, 47, 23-28.

Chakravarty, K. (1975) 'Regional Variation in Women's Employment : A Case Study of Five Temporal Studies in Rural India, 1951, 61, 71, ICSSR, *Programme of Women's* Studies (mimeo).

Cohen, R.E. (1980) 'Should Unions Participate in Quality of Work Life Activities', *The Canadian Scene*, 1(4), 7-12.

Construction Labour Market (1977-78) Five Studies Sponsored by National Buildings Organization, GOI.

Comer, L. (1974) '*Wedlocked Women*', Leads Feminist Books.

Cook, J. and Wall, T. (1980) 'New Work Attitude Measures of Trust, Organizational Commitment, and Personal Need Non-fulfilment', *Journal of Occupational Psybhology*, 53, 39-52.

Davis, L.E. and Cherns, A.B. (1975) '*The Quality of Working Life*', Vol. I and II, New York : Free Press.

Delamotte, Y. and Takezawa, S. (1984) '*QWL in International Perspective*', International Labour Organization, Geneva.

De, N.R. (1977) *Diffusion of Work System Redesign on Participative Design in a Large Complex Engineering Factory*, (*mimeo*), National Labour Institute, New Delhi.

De, N.R., (1977) '*Employee Motivation Through Work Redesign on Participative Lines in the Salary Saving Scheme of New Delhi Divisional Office of Life Insurance Corporation of India* (*mimeo*), National Labour Institute, New Delhi.

De, N.R. (1980) 'Redesign of Work System and Quality of Work Life', Joshi, N. C. and Kesary, V.G. (Eds.) *Readings in* managements. Allahabad : A.H. Wheeler.

De, N.R. (1975) '*Quality of Working Life : The Indian Scenario*' *National Labour Institute Bulletin*, (5), 1-10.

Durkheim E. (1947) 'De la Division Dutravil Social. The Division of Labour in Society (G. Simpson, Trans.)', New York: Free Press (Originally Published 1893).

Dunnette, M.D., Campbell, J and Haket, M. (1967) 'Factors Contributing to Job Satisfaction and Job Dissatisfaction in Six Occupationnl Groups', *Organizational Behaviour and Human Performance*, Vol. 2, 143-174.

'*Ekalavya*'—The Mobile Creches Annual, 1979.

Emery, F.E. and Emery, M. (1976) '*Participative Design*', Canberra, Centre for Continuing Education.

Emery, F.E. and Thorsrud E. (1979) '*Demacracy At Work*. Leiden : Martinus-Nijhoff.

Evenson, R.E. (1974) '*The Allocation of Women's Time : An Internationai Comparision*', Free Press.

Farouq, A. and Ali, M. (1975) '*The Hardworking Poors*' Dacca University, Dacca.

Festinger, L.A. (1957) '*A Theory of Cognitive Dissonance*', Evanston, III : Row, Peterson.

Galtung, J. (1975) '*Indicators Programme, Measuring World Development*', Oslo : University of Oslo.

Ganguly, O N. and Joseph, J.S. (1976) 'Quality of Working Life: Work Prospects and Aspirations of Young Workers in Air India, (Mimeo)', *Central Labour Institute*, Bombay.

George, S. (1984) 'Perception of Quality of Working Life : An Exploratory Study in Two Public Sector Undertakings. *An Unpublished M. Tech Dissertation*. I.I.T., Delhi.

Goldthorpe, J.H., Lockwood, D., Bechhofer, F. and Platt, J. (1968) '*The Affluent Worker : Industrial Attitudes and Behaviour*', Cambridge University Press.

Ghosh, S. and Kalra, S.K. (1982) 'Perceptual Differences in Quality of Work Life Factors', *Indian Journal of Training and Development*, 12 (3 and 4), 10-12.

Green, G, Cashman, J.F., Ginsburg, S. and Schiemann, W. (1977), 'Effects of Linking Pin Quality on the Quality of Working Life of Lower Participations', *Administrative Science Quarterly*, 22, 491-504.

Guest, R.H. (1979) Quality of Work Life-learning from Tany town, *Harvard Business Review*, 57(4), 76-87.

Hackman, J.R. and Oldham. G.R. (1980) *Work Redesign*. Reading, M.A. : Addison-Wesley.

Hackman, J.R. and Suttle, J. L. (1977) '*Improving Life at Work-Behavioural Science Approaches to Organizational Changes*', Good Year Publishing Company Inc., California, 414-416.

Hall, J. (1976) 'Subjective Measures of Quality of Life in Britain', 1971-75, *Social Trends*, No. 7, London: HMSO.

Hall, D.T. and Nougaim, K.E. (1968) 'An Examination of Maslow's Need Hierarchy in an Organizational Setting', *Organizational Behaviour and Human Performance*, Vol. 3, 12-35.

Hankiss, E. (1976) '*Quality of Life Models*', Budapest : Hungarian Academy of Sciences.

Hausser, D.L., Pecorella, P.A. and Wissler, A.L. (1977) '*Suney Guided Development : A Manual for Consultants*,' San Diego, C.A. : University Associates.

Heider, F. (1958) '*The Psychology of Interpersonal Relations*', New York, Wiley.

Heizel, M.F., Geodale, J.G. Joyner, R.C. and Burke, R.J. (1973) '*Development of a Quality of Working Life Questionnaire : Item Discrimination Study*', Department of Labour, Ottawa, Canada.

Harbst, P.G. (1979) 'Some Reflections on the Work Democratization Project' : The Process of Diffusion', L.E., Danis and A.B., Bherms (Eds.) *Readings in Organizational Design*, Los Angeles : UCLA, Centre for Quality of Working Life, 675-678.

Herrick, N. and Maccoby, M. (1972) Humanizing Work: A Priority Goal of the 1970's', *Paper presented at the International Conference on the Quality of Working Life*, Arden House, Harrison, New York.

Herzberg, F., Mausner, B. and Snyderman, B. (1956) '*The Motivation to Work*', (2nd ed.) New York : John Wiley.

Herzberg, F, (1968) 'One More Time: How do You Motivate Employees ? *Harvard Business Review*. 46, 53-62.

Hinkiss, E. (1978) 'Structural Variables in Cross-Cultural Research on the Quality of Life', *The Quality of Life—* Comparative Studies, (Ed.) Szalai, A. and Andrews, F.F., Sage Publication, California, 41-56.

Homons, G. (1961) '*Social Behaviour*', New York : Harcourt, Brace and Warld.

Horn, R.V. (1976) 'Quality of Working Life : The Social Indicator Approach', *Journal of Industrial Relations,* 143-254.

House, R.J. and Wigdor, L.A. (1967) 'Herzberg's Dual Factor Theory of Job Satisfaction and Motivation : A Review of the Evidence and a Criticism', *Personnel Psychology,* Vol. 20, 369-90.

Inkeles, A. and Diamond, L. (1960) 'Personal Development and National Development : A Cross-National Perspective' *The Quality of Life—Comparative Studies,* (Ed.) Szalai, A. and Andrews, F.F., Sage Publication, California, 73-109.

ILO : (1977) '*Report on Women Worker and Society : International Perspectives*' Geneva.

Jacques, E. (1961) '*Equitable Payment*', New York : Wiley

Jain, D. and Chand, M. (1980) '*Household Surveys*' ESCAP.

Jarett, I.M. (1976) '*Introduction in Key Factor Analysis*', Carbondale : Southern Lilinois University Press.

Joseph, J.S. (1978) 'Quality of Working Life (QWL) and *Job Attitudes of Indian Craftmen, Bombay Psychologists,* 11(1), 28-34.

Kalra, Kumar Satish and Ghosh, S. (1983) 'Quality of Working Life : Some Determinants : *Indian Journal of Management.*"

Katz, D. and Kahn, R.L. (1966) '*The Social Psychology of Organizations*', New York : John Wiley.

Kirsch, B.A. and Legermann, J.J. (1971) 'An Empirical Test of Robert Blauner's Ideas on Alienatlon in Work as Applied to Different Type Jobs in a White-collar Setting', *Sociology and Social Reseerch,* 56. 180-194.

Kohn, M.L. (1976) 'Occupational Structure and Alienation', *American Journal of Sociology*, Vol.82. 111-30.

Kohn, Melvin, L. and Schooler, C. (1973), 'Occupational Experience and Psychological Functioning: An Assessment of Reciprocal Effects, *American Sociological Review*, Vol. 38, 97-118.

Kossen Stair (1983) '*The Human Side of Organizations*', Third Edition, Harper and Row Publishers, New York, 263-255.

Lawler, E.E. (1971) '*Pay and Organizational Effcctiveness*', *Psychological Review*, New York: McGraw Hill.

Lengel, F. (1976) 'The Existence and Impact of Alienating Job Condition in the Hospital Medical Laboratory', *Unpublished Master's Project Report*, Wayne State University.

Lippitt, G.L. (1978) 'Quality of Working Life, Organization Renewal in Action', *Training and Development Journal* 32, (7), 410.

Lipset, S, Mastin (1960) '*Political Man*', Garden City, New York: Doubleday.

Livneh, A. (1978) 'Life-Cycle Approach to the Quality of Work Experience' *Dissertation Abstract International*' Vol. 39, Oct. 1978, 2578-A.

Lupton, T. (1975) 'Efficiency and the Quality of Work Life: The Technology of Reconciliation', *Organizational Dynamics* 4, (Autmn), 68-80.

Macy, B.A. and Mervis, P.H. (1976) 'A Methodology for Assessment of Equality of Working Life and Organizational Effectieness in Behavioural Economic Terms', *Administrative Science Quarterly* 21, 215-226.

Macy, B.A. (1979) 'Progress Report on the Bolivar Quality of Work Life Project', *Personnel Journal*, August, 527-559.

Malinowsky B. (1932) '*The Family among the Australian Aborigines: A Sociological Study*', London University of London Press.

Mallmann, C.A. (1977), Gaps in Mankind's Well-Being: Argentina as a Case Study, *Proceedings of the Symposium on the Scientific and Technological Gap in Latin America,'* London Nebraska: Institute for International Studies of the Unirersity of Nebraska.

Mallmann, C.A. (1977) '*Research Priorities and Holistic Knowicdge*' Bariloche: Fundacion Bariloche.

Marx, K. (1961) '*Economic and Philosophical Manuscripts of 1844* Mascow, Foreign Languages Publishing House.

Masini, E.B. (1975) '*Motivation and Proposal for a Research Study Project on Basic Needs and Changes of Values*, Rome: *WFSF*

Maslow, A.H. (1942) 'A Theory of Human Motivation', *Psychological Review*, Vol. 50, 370-96.

Maslow, A.H. (1954) '*Motivation and Personality*', New York, Harper anb Row.

Maslow, A.H. (1959) 'Cognition of Being in the Peak Experiences', *Journal of Genetic Psychology*, Vol. 94, 43-66.

Maslow, A.H. (1962) '*Towards a Psychology of Being*', New York: Van Nostrand.

Mathur, P, (1984) '*Job Demand Schedule Survey of Employment Experiences of IIT Gruduates*', Interium Report Submitted to IIT. Delhi.

Maurer, J.G. (1972) 'The Relationship of Perceived Task Attributes and Opportunity to Contribute to the Meaning of Work', *Paper Presented at the 19th International Meeting of Management Sciences*, Houston, Taxas.

Mayo, E. (1955) '*The Human Problems of an Industrial Civilization*', New York: MacMillan.

McGregor, D. (1960) '*The Human Side of Enterprise*', McGraw Hill Bcok Company-

Mahale, J. et.al. (1977) '*Basic Human Needs: A Framework for Action*'. Houston, Taxas: Center for Interactive Studies of the University of Houston.

Mead, M. (1975) '*Male and Female: A Study of the Sexes in a Changing World*', Hrmondsworth, Penguin,

Mehra, K.B. (1984) 'Relationship of Job Involvement to Background Factors : Perceived Importance of Needs, Need Satisfaction. *An Unpublished Dissertaiion, I.I.T., Delhi.*

Mehta, P. (1976) 'From Economism to Democratic Commitment, *The Role of Working Participation*', *Vikalpa*, 1 (4), 39-46.

Miller, G.A. (1967) 'Professionals in Bureaucracy: Alienation among Industrial Scientists and Engineers', *American Sociological Review*, 32, 755-768.

Miller, R.S. (Ed.) (1977) 'Participative Management, Quality Work Life and Job Enrichment', *Management Review* No.11, Park Ridge, N-J. Nayes Data Corporation.

Mitra, A. (1981) '*Participation of Women in Socio economic Indicators as Tools for Development Planning*. The case of India, Unesco, 51.

Monga, M.L. and Maggu, A. (1981) 'Quality of Work Life, a Study of Public Sector in India,' *ASCI Journal of Management* 10 (2) 115-137,

Moot, P.E. (1972) '*The Characteristics of Effective Organization*', New York: Harper and Row.

Mishra, D.S. (1985) 'Perception of Quality of Working Life: An Exploratory Study in Production and R&D units of two Public Sector Undertakings, *An Unpublished Disseriation*, IIT. Delhi.

Morse, N.C. and Weiss,R.S. (1955) 'The Function and Meaning of Work and the Job', *American Sociological Review*, 22, 191-198.

Murray, H.A. (1938) '*Explorations in Peasonaiity*', New York: Oxford University Press.

Nadler, D.A. (1977) '*Feedback and Organization Development Reading*', M.A. Addison-Wesley.

Nadler, D.A. and Lawler, E.E. (1983) 'Quality of Work Life: Perspectives and Directions. *Organizational Dynamics.*

Packard, T.R. (1981) 'QWL in Social Work Bureaucracy-Participation Performance and Job Satisfaction', *Dissertation Abstract International* Vol. 41, 5245-A.

Patchen, M. (1961) '*The Choice of Wage Comparisons*', Englewood Cliffs, N.J.: Prentice Hall.

Peartin, L.I. and Kohn, M.L. (1966) 'Social Class and Ethnic Roles', *American Sociotogical Review*, Vol. 31. 466-479.

Pomonis, B. and Baumgratel H. (1980) 'The Quality of Work Life Movement', *Human Futures*, 3 (3), 246-253.

Porter, L.W. (1954) '*Organizational Patterns of Managerial Attitudes and Performance*', New York : American Foundation for Management Research.

Rahman, Md. Azizan (1984) 'Quality of Working Life (QWL) as Perceived by the Industrial Shift Workers. *An Unpublished Doctoral Dissertation Osmania University*, Hyderabad.

Rezsohazy, R. (1978) 'Ways of Life and Social Change: Methodology of a Recurrent Investigation', *The Quality of Life Comparative Studies*, (Ed.) Szalai, A. and Andrews, F.F., Sage Publication, California, 201-210.

Sashkin, M. and Lengermann, J.J. (1984) 'Quality of Work Life Conditions/Feelings (Ed.) Pfeiffer, J.M. and Goldstein, L.D. (*1984*), *Annual Developing Human Resources*, 13th Annual, University Associates Inc., California, 131-144.

Sashkin, M, and Morris, W.C. (1984) *Organizational Behaviour and Management: Concepts and Experiences*', Beston, V.A: Reston Publishing.

Sayeed, O.B. and Sinha, P. (1981) 'QWL in Relation to Job Satisfaction and Performance in Two Organizations', *Managerial Psychology*, 2(1) 15-30.

Seashore, S.E. (1975) 'Defining and Measuring the Quality of Work Life, L.E. Davis and Cherns, A, (Eds.) *The Quality of Working Life*', (Vol. 1) New York: The Free Press.

Seáman, M. (1959) 'On the Meaning of Alienation,' *American Sociological Review*, 24, 783-791.

Siegel, S. (1956) '*Non-parametric Statistics for the Behavioural Sciences*', McGraw-Hill Kngakusha Ltd. Tokyo.

Singh, A.U. (1979) 'Quality of Working Life: A Professional Approach, *Industrial Relations.*

Singh, P. (1980) Motivational Profile and Quality of Corporate Work Life—A Case of Mismatch, *Paper Presented at the National Symposium on QWL Hyderabad*, July 25 and 26, (Symposium papers Vol. 4).

Sinha, G.P. and Ranade, S.N. (1975) '*Women Construction Workers Reports of Two Surveys* (*ICSSR*) Allied Publisher, New Delhi.

Sinha, P. (1982) 'Quality of Working Life and Quality of Life', *Indian Journal of Industrial Relations.* 17, (3). 373-394.

Sinha, P. and Sayeed, O.B. (1980) 'Measuring Quality of Working Life—Development of an Inventory, *Indian Journal of Social Work*, XLI (3), 220-226.

Singh, J.B, (1982) 'Improving Quality of Working Life in Indian Context', *Productivity*, 22, (4) 13-20.

Sinha, J.B.P, (1977) 'Quality of Working Life in the Indian Setting', *Journal of Social and Economic Studies*, 2, 235-247.

Smith, P.C., Kendall,L.M. and Hulin, C.L.(1969) '*The Measurement of Satisfaction in Work and Retirement: A Study of Attitude*', Chicago: Rand McNally.

Solomon, E.S. et.al.(1978) 'Unesco's Policy—Relevant Quality of Life Research Pragram. "*The Quality of Life—Comparative Studics* (Ed.) Szalai, A. and Andrews, F.F., Sage Publication, California, 223-233.

Sommerkamp, P.J. (1981) 'Effect of QWL Intervention of Paper Processing: Civil Service Workers Behaviours', *Dissertation Abstract International*, Vol. 42, 2271-A.

Sprin, P. (1975) 'Some Comments on the Quality of Working Life', *Journal of Occupational Psychology*, 48, 179-184.

Srivastava, S. et. al. (1975) '*Job Satisfaction and Productivity Cleveland*, Ohio, Case Western Reserve University, Deptt. of Organizational Behaviour, 73.

Stone, P.J. (1978) 'Organic Solidarlty and Life Quality Indicators', *The Quality of Life Comparative Studies* (Ed.) Szalai, A. and Andrews, F.F., Sage Publication, California, 212-219.

Szalai, A. (1978) 'The Meaning of Comparative Research on the Quality of Life', *The Quality of Life—Comparative Studies* (Ed.) Szalai, A. and Andrews, F.F., Sage Publication, California, 7-21.

Taylor, F. (1911) '*Scientific Management*', New York: Harper and Row.

Taylor, J.C. (1973) '*Concepts and Problems in Studies of the Quality of Working Life*: Graduate School of Management, UCLA.

Thorsrud, E. (1976) 'Democracy at the Work and Prospectives on the QWL in Scandinavia, *Research Studies*, No. 8, IILS, Geneva.

Towards Equality—*Report of the Committee on the Status of Women in India*, GOI, 1974.

Verwayen, H. (1978) 'The Specification and Measurement of the Quality of Life in OECD Countries, *The Quality of Life—Comparative Studies* (Ed.) Szalai, A. and Andrews, F.F. Sage Publication, California, 2.5-247.

Walker, K.F. (1975) 'Worker's Attitude—A Key to the Quality of Life', L.E. Davis and Cherns, A. *The Quality of Working Life*. Vol. I, The Free Press, 1-2.

Walton, R.F. (1975) 'Quality of Working Life : What it is ?' *Sloan Management Review*, 15 (1), 11-21.

Warr, P. and Wall, T. (1975) 'Work and Well-being', London: Penguin Book.

Weick, K.E. (1966) 'The Concept of Equity in the Perception of Pay', *Administrative Science Quarterly*, Vol. II, 414-439.

Werther, W.B. and Davisk, (1982) '*Personnel Management and Human Resources*', McGraw-Hill International, 65-83.

Whitsett, D.A. and Winalow, E.K. (1967) 'An Analysis of Studies Critical of Motivation—Hygiene Theory', *Personnel Psychology*, Vol. 20, 391-415.

Wilmoh, G.A. (1983) 'A Test of Discriminant Validiiy of Two Measures of Work Conditions and Two Measures of Effective responses to work', *Paper Presented at the Annual Meeting of the Southeastern Psychological Association*, Atlanta.

Wilson, N.A.B. (1973) 'On Quality of Working Life', *Manpower Paper 7, Department of Employment*, HMSO, London.

Index